CULTIVATING ROU

Shows how to set about making a fert... ... ...tamed plot, a patch of ground churned up by builders, or a neglected garden that has become a wilderness.

CULTIVATING ROUGH GROUND

Getting Neglected Plots Productive

by
Keith Wills

THORSONS PUBLISHERS LIMITED
Wellingborough, Northamptonshire

First published 1978

© KEITH WILLS 1978

This book is sold subject to the condition that it shall not, by way of trade or otherwise, be lent, re-sold, hired out, or otherwise circulated without the publisher's prior consent in any form of binding or cover other than that in which it is published and without a similar condition including this condition being imposed on the subsequent purchaser.

ISBN 0 7225 0486 1 (hardback)
ISBN 0 7225 0464 0 (paperback)

Photoset by
Specialised Offset Services Limited, Liverpool
and printed in Great Britain by
Weatherby Woolnough, Wellingborough, Northamptonshire
on paper made from 100% re-cycled fibre supplied by
P.F. Bingham Ltd., Croydon, Surrey

CONTENTS

Chapter		Page
1.	What this Book is About	7
2.	Assessing the Situation	12
3.	Tools and How to Use Them	27
4.	Setting to Work	51
5.	The First Year	73
6.	Future Years	86
	Some Useful Addresses	91
	Further Reading	92
	Index	93

1
WHAT THIS BOOK IS ABOUT

This book is written for all those thousands of people who every year move into a new house and find that they have taken on a garden as well. When I say 'garden', I use the word in a rather limited sense. The area around the house, enclosed by the fence and cluttered with what the builders have left behind, isn't really a garden. It's usually a mess, reminiscent of the Battle of the Somme, rutted by giant tyres, poisoned by cement and spilt diesel fuel, and full of buried horrors, like coils of wire, broken pipes, rusty nails, and thousands of half bricks. Often the top soil has been totally removed leaving you with inert, lifeless subsoil. To give credit where it's due, not all builders are so negligent as this. The very best always remove the top soil and put it back when all their operations are completed. I hope you have the good fortune to buy a house from such a paragon.

This book is also written for those other thousands who buy an older house, perhaps a country cottage with enough land to justify calling it a smallholding, and find, where a garden should be, a wilderness instead.

Both groups will include people who have never before lifted a spade in their lives. For these people, I have tried to give the most basic instructions in gardening methods. More experienced gardeners will pick out any information and advice they think useful. It's a book for the first year or so of your life in your new garden. It tells you how to make the best of what you've got and how to clear up the disasters left by other people. There are no learned discussions about the virtues and vices of particular plants, nor great lists of trees and shrubs that I think 'suitable' for particular situations.

The Organic Way

Throughout this book, you will find that I advocate nothing but organic methods. Only two weedkillers are tentatively suggested for certain limited situations. Otherwise, you will find the emphasis on killing weeds by digging them up rather than spraying them to death. The reasons for taking an organic approach are becoming much better known these days but I will re-state them briefly without trying to preach a sermon.

Organic gardening means gardening without using artificial fertilizers, and protecting plants by cunning and the use of biodegradable pesticides. It means feeding the soil with manure and compost, building up its fertility and thus the health and vigour of the plants grown in it. It means returning, as far as possible, what you take out of the soil. If all this sounds rather too noble and impractical, I should point out that organic methods served mankind well until about a hundred years ago, and they still serve the vast majority of people throughout the world to this day. Organic methods have kept the soil of China fertile through almost 5,000 years of cultivation. So, if you decide to do things the organic way, don't imagine you're joining a select band of cranks. You are joining the majority!

I can't pretend, as some writers have done, that organically-grown crops are absolutely free of pests and diseases. That would be almost as unnatural as having a crop completely destroyed by them. In nature, both conditions are rare. You will have some pests, some diseases but they will be on a moderate scale.

There is no denying that organic gardeners, just because they don't take the easy ways out offered by the more virulent herbicides and pesticides, do have to work harder. Making compost costs more effort than spreading fertilizer from a bag, digging out dandelions is harder work than spraying them with hormone weedkillers. This is something that you have to accept – that everyone, organic gardeners or not, will have to accept sooner or later, as the chemicals fail more and more to do what they should. You can at least feel saintly while you're bending your back. Sweat does no ecological damage.

Three Case Histories

These histories are part of my credentials for writing this book. They represent a great deal of bitter experience and are intended to give some idea of the problems you can meet in a new garden. The last two are fairly common situations.

Garden One
Standing at over 900 ft (290 metres) above sea-level, in an east-facing valley in the Lake District; steep hills to the south and north. The hill to the south, 2,000 ft (600 metres) high, cut off the sun completely for about a month in mid-winter. Because of its elevation, growth started much later in the garden than was general in the district. The other climatic problem was wind. The garden was quite hedgeless but even the best of hedges would have done little to stop the gusts ripping down from the steep slopes on either side. Light, gravel soil and a gradient produced good drainage, particularly necessary as the rainfall was nearly 100 inches (254cm) a year. This figure is about three times the national average and meant that one inch (2.5cm) of rain fell every three and a half days. The paths were good but the cultivated areas were completely overgrown.

The first task was to remove a dilapidated greenhouse before it fell on someone. This left a high concrete base wall, the area inside which I filled with turf, gradually taken off the vegetable garden over a month. An excellent crop of bush marrows was grown on the resultant mound. Flower beds were carefully weeded by hand – not the way I would choose to do it now. Many treasures were discovered, small rock plants hidden among the weeds, with bulbs below, including a small lily. One treasure went totally unregarded during our time in the garden – such was our ignorance. This was the rather uncommon parsley fern, which grew in every crack of the retaining walls. Diseased blackcurrant bushes were grubbed out and burnt. In the first summer, vegetable crops were miserable. This was, no doubt, due partly to my own ignorance but also to the washed-out condition of the soil. Constant rain quickly leached out any available nutrients. And I had aggravated the problem by removing the soil's natural cover, the turf.

The answer was to make compost, the chief ingredient of which was bracken, which could be cut in large quantities on the surrounding hillsides. Cut green, when still only two or three feet high, and mixed with urine and kitchen waste, this produced magnificent material, which was spread over the ground the following autumn and winter. A dressing of lime was also given. The following season the crops improved beyond recognition.

By far the heaviest work in this garden was stripping the turf and stacking it, and collecting compost material. Both these jobs were done without a barrow. The turf was moved a forkload at a time. The bracken was cut with a sickle, raked together with a broken rake and then stuffed into a stout old mattress cover. This huge sausage was then rolled down the hillside to a track, where it was slung across the crossbar of a bicycle and wheeled off to the compost heap. An old bike can take a surprising weight.

I saw the garden eighteen months after I had left it. Nature had completely taken over once more. All the cultivated areas had vanished under dense (compost-grown!) weeds and there were even a few seedling brooms showing. Nature was protecting the soil and even making some effort to return that piece of ground to its original forest cover.

Garden Two
A new house and a new garden, filled with builder's rubbish. One area of soil had been completely inverted – that is, the top soil had been buried beneath two feet of subsoil excavated from the foundations of the house. There were no paths, and the septic tank was inconveniently sited in the midst of the area best suited to vegetable growing. However, the soil was wonderful; heavy and fertile pasture, probably unbroken for over a hundred years. Once the rubbish had been cleared, I had the ground ploughed and rotavated. No problems, you may think. But, at that point, as soon as the ground was broken, my troubles began. The truth was that the garden was far too large for me to look after properly in the time I had available. I simply could not keep up with the weeds.

If I had cultivated only half of it and kept the rest in order with a scythe, I would have been much wiser. As it was, the garden never looked tidy. The crops were never clean but they grew well thanks only to the generous soil. It was rather like painting the Forth Bridge – as soon as I reached one end, I had to start work again at the other. There were few intervals for enjoyment. A little money invested in tidying tools like edging irons and clippers and even a small motor-mower would have been well-spent. A well-cut lawn edge has a great psychological effect. The garden may not be significantly improved but it looks one hundred per cent better.

Garden Three
This story has only just begun. The garden surrounds my present house. It has not been cultivated or looked after in any way for over a year. The vegetable garden is nothing but nettles and docks. There are paths hidden in rank weeds, and beneath one end of the vegetable garden I have discovered a disused septic tank filled with rubble. I am now busy knocking off the top courses of bricks and carting them, and the rubble, away. On the credit side, there is an apple-tree which, though ill-formed, bears delicious fruit; and many fine and mature shrubs. Someone, at some time, has put a lot of work and thought into this garden.

Already (this is November) part of the vegetable garden has been stripped of turf, dug over and planted with spring cabbages and broad beans. Couch grass is showing amongst them but this doesn't worry me because I know I shall conquer it with the hoe.

There is much to do but I think I can make everything in the garden lovely once more. I hope this book will help you to feel the same way.

2
ASSESSING THE SITUATION

So here you are in your new garden. The builders have left, the estate-agent or landlord has handed you the keys and it's all yours – every six-foot weed, every patch of brambles, every heap of builder's rubbish, every unkempt hedge and neglected fruit tree. What becomes of this piece of ground, whether the soil is the most perfect loam or nothing but stony rubbish, is up to you. Everything now depends on your strength, your skill and your knowledge, even to the extent of which advice you accept and which you ignore.

What is the first thing to do? The first thing to do is not to panic. Walk around, look at things, assess the situation. Don't make any decisions and certainly don't act on them. Simply find out what you've got.

Area
The first thing to find out is how much. An overgrown site looks very much smaller than a cultivated one. The weeds destroy the effect of distance. So, measure your plot with a long tape, or a two-metre measuring stick which you can easily make yourself. You can pace it out, but your measurements will not be as accurate or so valuable. Write your measurements down. Draw a plan. I suggest you buy a scientific notebook in which every other page consists of squared paper. The squares will help you to draw fairly accurate scale diagrams.

Aspect
Next, find out which way your plot faces. Ideally, it should face south because the south is where the sunlight comes from, and that's what makes the cabbages grow. If you have a compass the job is easy. If you haven't a compass, south is the direction from which the sun

shines for most of the day; or, if you face the sunset, south is more or less on your left. Of course, it's most likely that your plot surrounds the house and faces in all directions at once. In that case, the ground to the east and west will grow vegetables provided they're not shaded on the southerly side, but the ground which faces north may be too shady for them.

Slope
A slight slope to the south, so that the soil presents a larger area to the sun's rays every day, is very much to be desired. Steep slopes make vegetable growing more difficult because constantly-cultivated soil tends to move downwards. Growing fruit on a steep slope is not so much of a problem because fruit trees and bushes can (and ought to be) heavily mulched each year, so that the ground is never disturbed.

If you are obliged to grow vegetables on such a slope, it may be a good idea to terrace it in the same way as paddy fields are terraced in parts of Asia. This is hard work and not to be undertaken lightly. However, a sloping site does have one important advantage. Cold air always moves downwards, so that frost may pass you by and descend on your less fortunate neighbours at the foot of the hill. Market fruit growers know this and consequently prefer hillsides on which to plant their orchards. With this in mind, it is important not to have any high solid obstacle, such as a wall, that will prevent the freezing air draining away.

Height
Find out how high above sea-level your garden is. An Ordnance Survey one-inch map will tell you this. If you are above 600 feet (190 metres) fruit growing may be difficult. And, of course, the higher you are, the windier it is likely to be.

Prevailing Wind
Find the direction from which the wind blows most of the time. Trees on high ground will be bent away from the prevailing wind. In general, throughout the British Isles, winds blow most frequently from the south west, bringing in warm moist air from the Atlantic. Such air conditions are very beneficial to the growth of plants and are one of the factors that permit such a wide variety to be grown in this country.

Brushwood windbreak. Brushwood is best pushed into the ground at an acute angle. Two rows should be used, one slightly behind the other and sloping the opposite way.

Windbreak made from commercial half-inch plastic mesh attached to dahlia stakes (or stronger). Three foot high.

However, if the wind blows too hard and too long, growth suffers. This can be imperceptible or can take the extreme form of cabbages being blown out of the ground. If the site is unprotected, you will have to consider planting hedges – these are discussed in Chapter Five. But don't plant hedges in the first year in your new garden. Other things come first. Hedging plants are not cheap and it would be foolish to plant something so permanent in the wrong place. If winds are very strong, you can put up temporary windscreens. They need not last more than a year or two, and there are plastic meshes on the market especially designed for this purpose. Single plants, or small groups, can be protected by bundles of brushwood or pieces of polythene secured by canes.

Polythene windbreak. 500 gauge polythene is effective but it should be no higher than eighteen inches and must be well staked. Bury the bottom edge of the sheet.

Rainfall

It will come as a surprise to many people to learn that in most parts of the British Isles crops need to be irrigated, and heavily irrigated at that, at some time during the year. This is because most rain falls during the cool months when it is least needed. So, unless you live in a very wet area, such as the west coast, a reliable supply of water is something you may have to think about. Find out if there is an outside tap. Nothing is more irritating than having a hose dangling out of the kitchen window, so think seriously about arranging an outside supply. Even if you never have to water anything, there is nothing so useful for washing the mud off your boots.

If you have a spring or stream on your land, I suggest you consult your neighbours, both up and down street, as to local water rights. The trouble is, there is no such thing as free water. It is all under the control of the local water authority who will want to know if you propose *taking* water from 'your' spring or stream.

Drainage

This is not so complicated a question as it sounds, and most sites present very little difficulty. Nevertheless, look about for wet spots. Standing water, even in February, is something to be taken seriously. However, if your house has just been built, pools of standing water may be due to the impaction of the soil surface by the builder's heavy vehicles. Ordinary cultivation will soon cure this.

Wet ground on other sites may require you to investigate the drains. If the whole area seems generally damp and grows typical wet-ground plants like buttercups and rushes then you may have to consider draining it with trenches and land tiles. This requires a certain amount of expertise, but is not beyond an intelligent man with a strong back. Look for basic drainage techniques in Chapter Four. It is useful, in any case, to know where the house drains go. In country districts you are unlikely to be on main drainage, so find out where the septic tank is and where the drains that lead into it are. It would be disastrous and smelly to break these with a pick.

Existing Plants

Next to be noted down on your plan are the plants already growing in your new garden. Of course, if your house is absolutely new, there will be little or nothing at all. But, in a neglected garden there may be all sorts of treasures, so go carefully. Old cottage gardens, in particular, can be absolute gold mines of plants often considered lost to cultivation, so don't cut down, dig up or otherwise destroy anything you don't actually recognize as a weed. Your new neighbours can be very useful in this situation. As soon as they see you with a spade or pruners in your hand, they will come forward with remarks like: 'It used to be lovely. Isn't it a shame?' This is the moment to pump them for all the information you can get about the garden and its plants. Ask about the plants you don't recognize, about the varieties of fruit trees. Put a name to anything you can. Once you have a name you can look it up and find out what to do about it. Another thing to ask your neighbours is what varieties of vegetables *they* grow. You would be well advised to grow as they grow. Certain varieties suit certain soils.

Herbs, particularly those of the mint tribe (the mints themselves, thymes, marjoram), sage and lavender, survive quite well in the jungle conditions of the neglected garden. You will generally find them by treading on them, crushing the leaves and releasing their characteristic smells. Any plant with aromatic leaves is worth preserving. Look out as well for primroses and carnations. There may be varieties quite literally hundreds of years old, like the carnations Crimson Clove and Nutmeg Clove, or the primroses Quakeress and Mme de Pompadour.

Strawberries are great survivors as well, as are most soft fruits – such as blackcurrants, raspberries and the like. If the fruit bushes look vigorous and are still making new growth they will probably be worth preserving, otherwise throw them out and buy strong young stock. Look particularly carefully at blackcurrants or have someone who knows about them look for you. Old blackcurrants are prone to a nasty condition called 'big bud', which is caused by microscopic insects called blackcurrant gall mites. The condition, as its name suggests, is characterized by unusually large buds. The gall mite is also the carrier of a virus disease called reversion. Bushes with reversion suffer from distorted growth and have darker-coloured leaves. The leaves also take on an unbalanced shape, that is, one side looks different from the other. Look in any good book about fruit growing (see Further Reading) for photographs. If you find your bushes suffering from either of these conditions, it is your duty to dig them up and burn them before the infection spreads to the bushes in your neighbour's garden.

You may find much ground covered by brambles. If the plants are all over the place and seem distributed randomly, then they are no doubt seedlings and you can destroy them with a clear conscience. However, if they seem to have been planted to a pattern, hesitate. They may be some worthwhile variety, like Himalaya Giant.

Another plant which shows itself quickly in the neglected garden is the elderberry. Don't get rid of them all. Save a couple for the blossom and the wine. Old country people used to regard the elderberry as a lucky plant and were most reluctant to cut one down close to their homes.

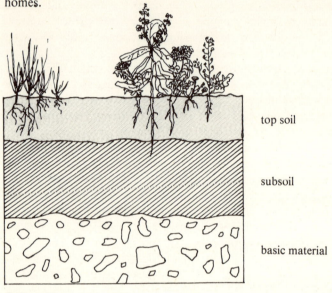

Soil profile.

Assessing Your Soil

Many gardeners get by for years without knowing much more about their soil beyond describing it as 'loam' or 'heavy'. They would do very much better if they knew exactly what they were up against. Soils differ and it is not much use treating clay as though it were sand.

In this section I shall explain simply what exactly is meant by such terms as 'loam' and 'clay' and how you can assess the texture, actual and potential fertility, drainage and lime content of your soil.

You can call in an expert to do this from the Agricultural Development and Advisory Service or from a private firm, but it will cost you money. It is best to do the job yourself, for you will learn much more in the process than the analyst's report could tell you.

The first thing to do is to get a spade and dig a hole three feet deep and wide enough for you to see the sides clearly. You will then be able to observe what is called the soil profile, which is nothing more than a vertical cross-section (a typical one we hope) of the soil in your garden. The soil profile you reveal will be unique, of course, but it will probably be quite like some other fairly typical profiles. The illustration below is idealized but shows you what to look for.

The top layer, as you might expect, is called the top soil. This should be appreciably darker than the lower levels because it contains, or should contain, rotting organic matter and (we hope) manure and compost. This matter of colour is important because not only does darkness indicate the level of organic matter, or humus, it also means that the soil will absorb the sun's rays more readily and so warm up more quickly in the spring. This quality is vital for early growth.

The top soil contains most of the millions of living organisms essential to fertility. Most of them are invisible, but you should see worms; and the more you see the better. Worms eat soil and, in passing it through their guts, increase its fertility. They also dig thousands of feet of air passages. Healthy roots need air to breathe, and a good population of worms ensures they get it.

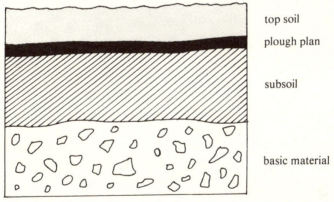

Plough pan.

Obviously, the more top soil you have the better. In the Fens, where most of the market vegetables in Britain are grown, the rich top soil goes on down for as much as ten or twelve feet. However, don't be discouraged if your own top soil isn't quite so good. The shallowest, poorest soil can be improved by diligent cultivation and plenty of muck.

If your new garden has been made from cultivated farm-land, there may be what is called a plough pan between the top soil and the layer below it; the subsoil. This pan, a thin layer of hard material, sometimes almost iron-hard, is caused by the weight and pressure of the plough passing over it at the same depth year after year. Pans can also be caused by the interaction of chemicals in the soil.

A pan must be broken or it will interfere seriously with growth – particularly with those deep roots which bring up essential minerals from far down in the subsoil. Farmers use a special plough called a sub-soiler for this job. If you have more than a $\frac{1}{2}$-acre of ground, you may be justified in getting a contractor to do the work for you. Otherwise, I'm afraid, it's a case of hard work and blisters with pick and spade.

Below the top soil, predictably enough, lies the subsoil. This generally consists of the basic mineral material out of which the top soil is made. It tends to be much lighter in colour, because it contains much less organic matter. Look for roots and note how far down they penetrate. Take particular note of the texture of the subsoil. On this will depend the drainage of the top soil. A clay subsoil tends to make the soil above too wet, however good the texture of the top soil may be. Yellow or grey clays are worst in this respect. These colours indicate an absence of air. On the other hand, a gravel or sand subsoil tends to make the top soil dry out too quickly.

Below the subsoil, if you reach that far, you meet what can hardly be classed as soil at all – indeed, it may be solid rock; beds of gravel; slabs of limestone; impenetrable clay. What it is will affect the growth of plants but there's nothing the average gardener can do to change it.

In a garden surrounding a new house, you sometimes come across a situation where the builders, in levelling a sloping site to make foundations, have dragged subsoil on top of the top soil and left it there. There is not much you can do about this beyond digging as deeply as you can and mixing the two layers together. Eventually, with the addition of much muck, and the natural weathering of the subsoil, where it is exposed to wind, rain and frost, you may have a good deep bed of much improved soil. In the meantime, don't expect too much of what is growing in it.

There are three final things you can do before you fill in the hole. First, take out a trowelful of soil from each layer and put it aside for assessment. Secondly, I suggest you make a drawing of the profile, giving measurements and noting the textures of the various levels. This may strike you as being unnecessarily scientific, but I believe that nothing will be of more value to you in future years than a well-filled notebook. Thirdly, fill the hole with water and see how quickly it drains away. If it vanishes in a few hours, then all is well. If it doesn't, take advice and consult the section on drainage in Chapter Four.

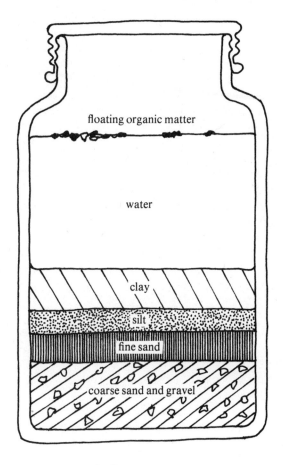

Sediment soil test.

Testing for Soil Type

You can get an accurate idea of your soil type by the following simple test. Take a small quantity of dry soil, making sure it is a representative sample, and put about four tablespoonsful in the bottom of a screw-capped straight-sided 2lb jam jar. Fill the jar almost full of water and screw on the lid. Shake the jar vigorously, so that the soil completely dissolves in the water. Leave the jar where it will be undisturbed overnight.

When you come to inspect the jar you will find that the soil particles of different sizes have settled at different levels – coarse sands and gravels at the bottom, fine sand above them, silt above the sand and clay on top. There should be a distinct line between each layer, and floating on top of the water, there should be a little raft of organic matter. The bigger the raft, the better, although this is not an accurate test of the soil's humus content. The proportions of sand, silt and clay will help you to give a name to your soil.

TABLE OF SOIL TYPES

Soil Type	Constituent %		
	Sand	Silt	Clay
Sand	85	10	5
Sandy loam	60	25	15
Loam	45	35	20
Silty loam	20	60	20
Clay loam	30	35	35
Clay	25	30	45

From the above, you will see that a sandy soil does not consist of sand alone, and that a clay soil is not exclusively clay. Each soil is different and you must not expect your soil to conform exactly to the indications given in the table.

A quicker way to assess soil is to pick it up and feel it. A sandy soil feels gritty, a silt or loamy soil feels silky, while clay is sticky and can be moulded with the fingers – on the heaviest clays it can almost be made into a pot! Try rolling the soil into a ball. A sandy soil will not hold that shape at all. A loamy sand will just hold together. A loamy clay will hold the ball shape and can be rolled out to form a cylinder. With clay, you can extend the cylinder into a worm and even form a circle with it.

Characteristics of Different Soil Types

A sandy soil drains quickly, warms quickly in the spring but can starve plants later in the year as its reserves of moisture and nutrients become depleted. Sandy soils are hungry soils – they demand heavy dressings of compost or manure to keep them productive. At the other extreme, clay soils are cold and slow-draining but are very slow to dry out. They are hard to work but can reward with high yields. They are hungry for manure in another sense – the organic matter opens the soil and lets in the vital air. Between the two lie the loams which are generally the best soils to have, the easiest to manage and, over a wide range of crops, the most productive.

The Importance of Lime

This is an important topic but one which is often neglected. Many gardeners would be amazed by the difference the correct level of lime in their soil would make to their efforts.

Plants need lime, but some plants need more lime than others. Lime, (or other forms of calcium, like chalk) is needed by plants in two chief ways. First, as a food. Cabbages, for instance, take up calcium and pass it on to us when we eat them. Needless to say we need calcium to build bones. Cows get the calcium, which they pass on in such generous quantities in milk, from grass. Secondly, plants need lime to produce the conditions they like in the soil in which they grow. Put simply, lime acts as a kind of catalyst which enables plants to take up the nutrients they need from the soil. Too much lime, or too little, and the plant foods become insoluble and thus unavailable.

Lime improves the texture of the soil. This is particularly noticeable on clay soils, where lime causes the minute clay particles to cling together or 'flocculate' in what are called crumbs. The bacteria which produce nitrates (essential to vigorous leaf growth) in the soil, work better in less acid soil conditions. Liming increases the population of earth worms, and it reduces the danger of club root, a debilitating disease of the cabbage family which is most common on acid soils.

Acidity and Alkalinity

Perhaps the easiest way to define these much-used terms is to give examples of soils which can reasonably be expected to be either acid or alkaline. A peat moor is acid. Peat moors occur in districts of high rainfall. The rain washes the lime away. Without lime, the dead vegetation cannot rot and so peat forms. Heathers are a characteristic peat moor and acid soil plant, as well as conifers, furzes, birch trees and foxgloves. On acid soils very little clover grows. The grass itself will be of poor quality, not the dense, luscious growth that you will see in a well-manured and well-limed pasture. In other people's gardens, on acid soils, you will see rhododendrons and azaleas growing.

Typical alkaline soils over-lie chalk. The stones in the fields tend to be white. Typical wild plants are beech, old man's beard (the native, wild clematis) dogwood and ash.

Looking for features of this kind will help you to make an informed guess. To know for sure, you must make a test. Soil testing kits are readily available, easy to use and cheap. You will, of course, follow the instructions for the particular kit you buy but, in general, the idea is to take samples of dry soil from all over your garden, mix them together and put a small quantity in a test tube. Next, a measured amount of reactive liquid is added and the test tube is corked and shaken. The fluid, as it mixes and reacts with the lime in the soil, changes colour. You compare the colour with the colours on a chart that comes with the kit, and from that you can find out the degree of acidity or alkalinity of your soil. I suggest you make three tests, taking different samples each time.

It may be that your test kit will produce an answer like 'pH 6.5'. This term 'pH' is something you will encounter a great deal in gardening and farming literature, so it had better be explained.

Put in the simplest possible way, pH is the scale on which the amount of lime in soil is measured. It means much more than that to a chemist, but that need not concern us here, and although it has a precise scientific meaning, it is quite easy to understand.

The mid-point of the scale is pH 7. This is neutrality, neither acid nor alkaline. It is the pH of pure, distilled water. Numbers below it, such as pH 6, indicate acidity; numbers above it, such as pH 8, indicate alkalinity. An important point to note about the scale is that it is logarithmic. That is pH 5 is ten times more acid than pH 6. In the same way, pH 8 is ten times more alkaline than pH 7.

Soil test kit.

There is not enough space in this book to give the pH preferences of a large number of plants, so consult the largest possible gardening dictionary for that kind of information. However, as far as vegetables are concerned, the following suggestions may be useful. Most common vegetables do well at about pH 6.5. The cabbage family, tolerate and, indeed, thrive under alkaline conditions, so that in an ordinary three-course rotation the ground set apart for them is always limed. Conversely the ground intended for potatoes is never limed. Too much lime causes an unpleasant-looking skin condition called scab.

Liming Materials

The two most generally available liming materials are ground limestone, or chalk, and hydrated lime. The ground materials are coarser and have a more lasting effect. Hydrated lime is very fine and should be handled with care and not, if possible, in windy weather. Watch out for your eyes. These materials are cheapest when bought in quantity. They do not deteriorate if stored in a dry place. A third material, gypsum, is wonderful stuff for breaking up clay. It is rather hard to get hold of but mushroom growers use it, so you could approach them. As to the correct quantity to apply, consult the table below.

LIME APPLICATION TABLE

pH	Ounces per square yard of hydrated lime needed to bring the soil pH to 6.5 (suitable for most vegetables)				
	sand	light loam	medium loam	heavy loam	clay or peat
4.5	8	10	12	14	16—18
5.0	6½	8	10	12	14—15
5.5	5½	7	8	10	11—13
6.0	5	6	6½	7	9—10
6.5	—	—	—	—	—

Lime should be spread as long as possible before growing the crop, so that it can take full effect. It should be spread evenly and then dug in to ensure an even distribution through the soil. Because liming speeds up the decomposition of organic matter and the release of nutrients, it should always be accompanied by a proper programme of feeding and manuring.

3
TOOLS AND HOW TO USE THEM

Making a garden out of your newly-acquired jungle will probably be the heaviest work you will do in all your life, so you must have the right tools for the job. Once you have matched the work to the tool life becomes very much easier. And you must make sure that the tool itself will unfailingly do what is asked of it. This means buying or hiring quality. This can be expensive but necessarily so. There is no point in spending your money on tools that bend, snap, buckle or otherwise fail. A bad tool has a perversity all its own and will usually choose to fail at five o'clock on a Saturday evening when it is too late to get hold of a replacement.

Not only must you buy quality but the tools must be the right size and weight for *you* to use. Pick up the implements while you are in the shop. Heft them in your hand. If the handle seems too long, if it feels too heavy, don't be shy, say so. Most shop assistants will be only too pleased to try and find you the right thing. If they are not, go to another shop.

Of course, if you have had a garden before, you will already have many of the tools discussed in this chapter. Some of the heavier tools and machines may only be needed for a few days. Most of these can be borrowed or hired. I suggest you consult the yellow pages in the telephone directory under 'Hire Contractors, Tools' to find out who leases tools near you. A quite surprising variety can be hired these days. Look in the same place under 'Contractor's Plant Hire' or 'Agricultural Contractors' if you have to hire a man with a plough or a rotavator or some heavy machine that you cannot handle yourself.

The following tables list all the tools you are likely to need, their current (1977) prices, and if they can be hired and at what rate. The tables are as comprehensive as I can make them and also list many tools, like hoes, that you will need to maintain, rather than make your

TABLE OF TOOLS

	Price to Buy £	Price to Hire £
Hand Tools		
Bow saw	3.50	50p per 2 days
'Chillington' hoe	6.00	
Fork	8.00-14.00	
Grass hook	2.50	
Hay rake	4.50	
Hedge clipper	2.50-8.50	
Hoe	2.50	
Hone	1.30	
Mattock	5.00-6.00	
Pick axe	5.00-6.00	50p per 2 days
Post-hole borer	22.00	1.00 per 2 days
Pruning saw	3.50	
Rake	3.00-6.00	
Scythe	14.00	
Shovel	5.00-6.00	50p per 2 days
Sickle	4.50	
Slasher	10.00	
Spade	8.00-14.00	
Three-tined cultivator	2.50-6.50	
Tree pruners	10.00	
Machinery etc.		
Flamegun	24.00	1.40 per day
Hedge clipper (electric)	25.00-65.00	3.00 per day
(petrol)	110.00	6.00 per day
Rotavator (wheel-driven)	400.00-1,200.00	
(tine-driven)	170.00-250.00	6.00-9.00 per day
Rotary mower	100.00	4.00-7.00 per day
Scrub cutter	150.00	4.00-5.00 per day
Other items		
Bucket	2.00	
Weedsheet	3.00	
Wheelbarrow	15.00	75p per 2 days

garden. It is a guide only. There is no need to rush out and buy every tool mentioned. None of the prices or rates are definitive.

The Human Engine

This is the machine that powers or guides all the other tools. You cannot buy a better-quality one if you are dissatisfied with the one you have got. In this section I shall suggest ways to get the best out of your body without putting it under undue strain.

It is unfortunately true that the way we live now has made most of us rather less fit for hard work than our parents and grandparents. We all know why: we ride instead of walk, we have machines to do tedious, repetitive tasks for us, even the smallest lawn is mown by a little electric machine. Heart disease, which many doctors associate with lack of exercise, is reaching epidemic proportions in the Western world. So consider carefully: are you fit enough to finish the job?

If you have ever had heart disease; or any serious illness within the last six months, go to your doctor, tell him what you hope to do and ask his advice.

You may think I'm being over-emphatic about this but until you have done it, you won't believe what hard work it is to push a barrow-load of broken bricks over rough ground, how hard it is to dig out and remove a tree-stump or a boulder, how exhausting it is digging sticky yellow clay.

But there is a more cheerful side to all this. So long as you take it easy at first, your body will learn how to cope with the strain. You will develop muscles, skills, the knack of work. Don't be in a hurry, even though spring is on the way. Don't push yourself to the limit. Stop when you begin to feel tired.

Much of the fatigue involved with this kind of heavy work is mental. It is a good plan, and one that I have always found helpful, to stop when you are very bored and go and do something more interesting for half an hour.

It is very important to look after your hands. Unless you already work with them they will not have developed thick protective callouses or 'segs'. So, to avoid blisters, you must wear gloves; if possible the thick leather ones worn by forestry and building workers. Avoid the plastic-covered type. They will make your hands sweat and they nearly always crack at the joint between the thumb and index finger. Washing-up gloves are no good at all. Don't do anything with your hands if you can do it with a tool. Don't scrabble in the soil to pick up broken bricks. Use a fork. And you will find that you can pick up and throw quite large stones with a shovel. If you do get a blister, don't prick it with what you fondly imagine to be a sterilized needle. Cover it with a well-padded wound dressing.

Look after your feet as well. If it is very wet you will have to wear rubber boots, in which case I advise you not to go on the ground at all. Nothing is more damaging to the structure of the soil than to trample about on it in wet weather. Otherwise, ordinary work boots are the most practical. The best have thick, cleated rubber soles and steel toe-caps. These last may save you a few toes one day if you make a silly mistake with a rotavator. If you think you are going to do much kneeling, you can buy knee-pads, but a wad of newspaper stuffed in a fertiliser sack is cheaper.

During all this hard work you are almost bound to cut yourself, and the wound will certainly be dirty. The risk is that you can be infected with tetanus or 'lockjaw', which is an extremely unpleasant and often fatal disease. The tetanus bacillus lives in the intestines of grazing animals and passes to the soil by their droppings. So, even if your new garden has never had a cow grazing it, it may have been mucked with animal manure and the bacillus will be present in the soil. If you haven't been protected previously (anti-tetanus jabs are given after quite minor accidents) please see your doctor and have a series of injections. The first is followed by another after six weeks and the final one after six months. They are free and they may save your life.

A final piece of quasi-medical advice for those unfortunate city-bred people who may not know what every three-year-old country child does; nettle stings are best relieved by rubbing the place with a dock-leaf.

The Mechanics of Work
The human body was not evolved to do heavy labour. Those peoples who are still nomadic hunter-gatherers, such as the Australian Aborigines and the Kalahari Bushmen, remind us of how our common ancestors spent their lives for millions and millions of years. Underneath our clothes and layers of civilized fat, we still have the bodies of people who spent their days in constant movement in the search for food. It is no accident that the strongest muscles in our bodies are in our thighs. Work, digging the ground, raising stones to build houses, excavating irrigation ditches, are all activities that have

arrived pretty late in our evolutionary history. Our bodies have adapted very little to these tasks. The pyramids were raised by human ingenuity as much as by sweat. In other words, there is usually an easy way to do something hard if only you can think of it.

How to Lift
As mentioned, the strongest muscles in your body are in your thighs, so use them rather than those weaker ones in your back and arms. Suppose you have to lift a large stone, or a concrete block. Crouch down, bending at the knees, not at the waist and keep your back straight. Your spinal column is a very vulnerable mechanism. Once you have the stone in your hands, or better still cradled in your arms, straighten your legs. Transfer the stone to a barrow as soon as you can. If you cannot lift the stone at all try to get a shovel under it. Once you have shifted the stone onto the blade of the shovel, you can use the shovel as a kind of sledge to drag it away.

How to lift heavy items.

Try to avoid carrying heavy objects any distance. But if you have to, get whatever it is on to your shoulder so that the load is transmitted down through your spine in a straight line. Carrying something heavy in your arms at hip or waist level is asking for trouble.

Long heavy objects, such as planks, scaffold poles or the branches of trees are best carried on the shoulder. Stand at one end of the plank, crouch down and lift it to chest level in the way already described. Now, lift the end of the plank above your shoulder and walk slowly towards the centre of the plank, shifting your grip as you go. When you reach the centre of the plank (and its centre of balance), the end facing you will swing up into the air and all you have to do is walk away with it.

If you encounter something you cannot move, try using a lever of some kind. Even the lightest and most slack-muscled person can exert extraordinary force if he or she has a lever long enough. Fence-posts, crowbars, pieces of four-by-two timber left by the builders, anything will do. It is important to get the fulcrum (what the lever moves over), as close to the lifted object as possible.

Cars can be made to move heavy objects with a stout rope or wire cable, if they are fitted with a substantial tow-bar, but don't try to move anything by tying it to your bumper. With most modern cars you will leave the bumper behind as soon as you let in the clutch. If you can, make a road for the tree-stump or boulder with planks or sheets of corrugated iron roofing. The car's jack can be pressed into service as well. Probably the ideal tool for moving heavy objects, with muscle-power only, is a winch. The important point with these is to make sure that the winch is securely anchored before you apply pressure.

TOOLS FOR BREAKING THE GROUND

Spades

The spade is the gardener's basic tool. You can do without a lot of things in a garden but you cannot do without a spade. If you have to buy one, be sure to buy the best. And the best, in my opinion, is a spade with a stainless steel blade to which the soil will not stick; it will have a plastic-covered steel shaft that will never break; the grip will be a D or Y pattern. Some people prefer the T pattern, but it is less strong and is just marvellous for hooking onto your coat pocket and ripping it off as you dig. If you find this too expensive (and it will be expensive!) and have to settle for less, look for strength, backed by a well-known name. Some manufacturers produce spades with a variety of handle-lengths. One type of spade is especially made for digging clay. Its edge is divided into four sharp triangular points, which, it is claimed, make penetration of the clay easier.

Take it easy when you dig, remembering always that it is a most unnatural activity. Take small slices (or 'spits') of earth at a time. Always use your instep and those wonderfully-strong thigh muscles to push the blade into the earth. You can always tell an absolute beginner by the way he swings the spade high and stabs it down as though it were an assegai!

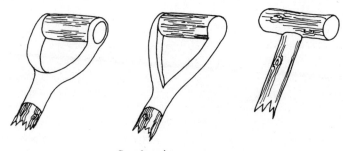

Spade grip patterns.

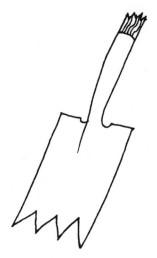

Clay digging spade.

Forks

Look for the same standards of construction in forks. If anything, a fork tends to be used most in a new garden because it is more useful for weeding than a spade. There are two sorts of digging-fork, round and flat-tined, with little to choose between them. The flat-tined is meant for digging potatoes but will do for most other jobs. A 'tine', for the uninitiated, is a prong. The border fork, a smaller and lighter version of the digging fork, is often preferred by women. It is not as strong, so even though its lightness and handiness may suit you, try not to use it for heavy work.

If you have a lot of manure, hay, straw or anything bulky and fibrous to move, then a muck-fork is the best tool. This is the same length as a digging-fork but the head is wider with four long, slender, slightly-curved tines.

Shovels

Shovels come in two patterns, the square-mouth and the round-mouth. The square-mouth, with a wide oblong blade, is used for moving large quantities of loose material like earth, gravel and sand. It is not designed for digging. If you have to move a heap of sand, shovel it away from the bottom, don't stab at the top of the heap. Place the blade at the foot of the heap and holding the grip of the shovel against your thigh (those thighs again!), crouch and use all your weight and strength to push it under the sand. This is much more economical of effort than using your arms alone. Swing the loaded shovel from the hip. You will be surprised how far you can throw the sand in this way.

Square mouth and round mouth shovels.

Sand heaped on bare earth, rather than a hard surface, can be difficult to shovel because the earth prevents the blade of the shovel from sliding cleanly beneath the sand. You can overcome this problem by pushing some smooth rigid material, such as a sheet of plywood or corrugated iron into the base of the heap. The sand will fall down on to it where it can be shovelled up easily.

The round mouth pattern of shovel has a blade shaped like the spades in a pack of cards. Navvies use it for digging trenches. It is much better for digging rough, stony ground than an ordinary spade.

Pickaxes
The pick is a tool for strong men. It is used for breaking stony ground where nothing else will do. It will break up tarmacadam, crumbling concrete paths and your back if you use it the wrong way. Both ends should be sharp. A pick is heavy, so do not try to lift it up and swing it back over your shoulder before you strike. Bend your back and your knees and take short stabbing pecks at the work. Rest frequently and watch out for your toes.

Mattocks
A mattock is similar to a pick, except that one of its blades is like a stubby axe and the other is adze or scoop-shaped. It is good for digging out tree-roots, breaking heavy clods, digging out drainage-ditches and all sorts of things. It is, in fact, an absolutely essential tool for breaking new ground. It is not the sort of tool you will use much once your garden is established. It is very easily borrowed in country districts.

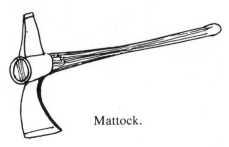
Mattock.

Three, or Multi-tined Cultivators

This is the best tool for breaking the clods left by digging or ploughing. A fork will do it as well but not so quickly. These tools have three or five tines arranged in an arrow-head formation. Sometimes the width of tillage can be adjusted. They are very good for cultivating between such widely-spaced crops as peas and brussels sprouts.

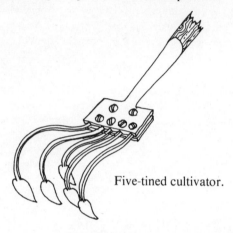

Five-tined cultivator.

Rakes

The best rakes are those with the back and tines machined out of a single piece of steel. In the cheaper sorts, the tines, which are riveted through the back, tend to work loose. A rake need be no wider than 30cm (1foot). Wider ones are rather clumsy and tiring to use. For cut grass, a wooden hay-rake or a spring-tined lawn rake is useful. If necessary, you can make do with an ordinary rake and a fork.

Hoes

There are two basic types. The dutch, which you use walking backwards holding the implement at hip-level, is the most useful for general work in the garden. The draw hoe is not much more than a kind of very light mattock. It is used mainly for earthing up potatoes and singling long rows of root crops. For light work between closely-spaced plants, there is the onion hoe. It is no more than a short-handled draw hoe with a long, swan-necked tang. Another type, intermediate in weight between a draw hoe and a mattock, has just recently come on to the market. For many years, this sort of tool – a 'Chillington' hoe – has been exported to Africa and Asia, where it is more popular as a cultivating tool than a spade.

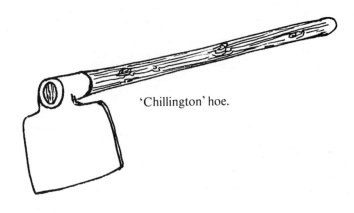

'Chillington' hoe.

CARRYING TOOLS

Barrows

You must have a barrow. Serious but quick work is impossible without it. I know the Chinese build gigantic dams using nothing but spades and baskets, but they would do the job better with a few thousand barrows. For most situations, the best kind of barrow is the sort that navvies use on building sites. It is lighter than a wooden one, better balanced, and will take an enormous amount of punishment. Most importantly, it has a big pneumatic wheel which will carry a load over rough ground with the greatest of ease.

Do not even contemplate heavy work with a barrow equipped with a solid, narrow tyre. Such barrows are only effective on a hard surface. If you are doing a repetitive job, it is worthwhile to make a roadway of planks. On very rough ground, with a heavy load, the best technique is to face the load and walk slowly backwards. You can get a barrow up a few steps this way.

There are larger barrows, with two pneumatic wheels. They will carry more, of course, but they are not as manoeuvrable as the ordinary kind.

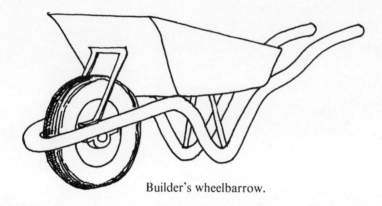
Builder's wheelbarrow.

Buckets
These are essential. The galvanized type or the heavy plastic kind will take most punishment. Plastic handles tend to break or become loose very easily, so make sure that they are metal and firmly secured.

Weedsheets
These are usually sheets of woven plastic material, about five feet square with a handle at each corner. Once you have piled your grass-cuttings or weeds in the centre of the sheet, you gather in each corner, grasp all four firmly together and cart the lot off over your shoulder. Useful in some situations, but I prefer a barrow myself.

TOOLS FOR CONQUERING THE JUNGLE
Scythe
By a scythe, I mean the usual English pattern, with its beautifully curved shaft, or the Aberdeen pattern with its complex Y-shaped shaft, used in parts of Scotland. I don't mean a grass-hook stuck on the end of something like the shaft of a golf-club. These are dangerous and tiring implements.

Using a scythe is one of those tasks which is much better demonstrated than described but in case you don't know some old labourer who will show you how, I shall do my best to give you a few tips. First of all, scything is not hard work. The easy, swinging motion, the shape of the blade and its keen edge do all the work. Once you have the knack you will find scything a pleasure. The scythe is one of the most perfectly adapted tools in existence.

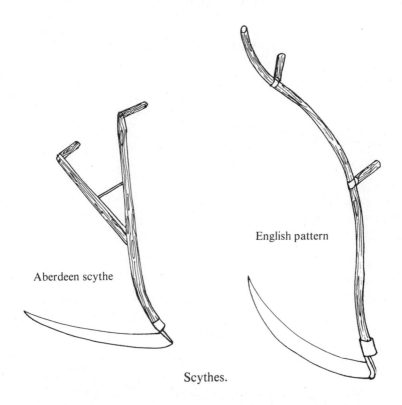

Aberdeen scythe

English pattern

Scythes.

The curved cutting edge of the blade must be perfectly even, without waves or dents and without a broken point to push the grass away from the edge. Old scythes sometimes get like this, so don't have anything to do with them, unless you actually enjoy working unnecessarily hard. A new blade will, of course, be perfectly shaped. For rough stuff, you can buy what is called a 'bramble' blade.

Sharpen a scythe with a hone; the rougher the work, the rougher the hone. Be very careful of your forefinger and thumb. Hold the scythe with the blade uppermost and steady the shaft with your knee and foot so that the tip of the blade points away from you and the cutting edge faces the ground. Steadying the blade with your left hand, stroke each side of the edge in turn, working your way to the tip. Make short strokes and, until you have the knack, do it slowly. Be sure that each stroke goes forward to the tip, never backwards. These forward strokes create hundreds of tiny serrations, like the teeth of a saw.

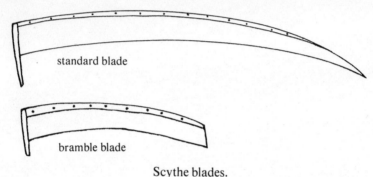

Scythe blades.

With your right hand on the lower handle, and your left on the upper, start scything at the bottom left-hand corner of the piece you intend to mow and work your way clockwise round it. Take a gentle, short swing. Keep the heel of the blade as low to the ground as you can. The lower you sweep, the more the grass resists and the easier it is to cut. Take a narrow cut each time, no wider than a foot. You should try to cut a long, narrow half-moon shape in the grass in front of you. At each stroke, what you have cut (the swath) should fall to your left-hand side where it won't impede the next stroke.

In skilled hands a scythe can be made to cut quite short grass, even a lawn. Before the invention of the cylinder mower all lawns were cut in this way.

Grass-hook

A grass-hook is for the corners where a scythe cannot go. It is harder work to use because you have to bend. Like a scythe, it is an exclusively right-handed tool. A left-hander can use a grass-hook if he makes a cut rather like a tennis-player playing a backhand shot, but it is not very safe. When using a grass-hook, carry a stick and hold it in front of your left shin as you work.

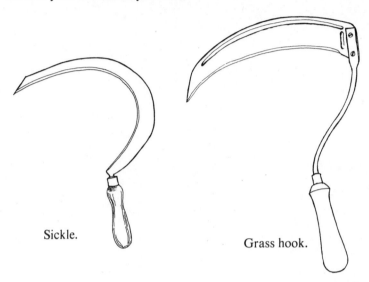

Sickle.

Grass hook.

Sickle
A sickle can do what a grass-hook can do but it can also tackle things like saplings and brambles. Because of the more pronounced curve of the blade, it has to be sharpened more carefully than the preceding tools.

Billhooks and Slashers
There are so many regional patterns of this kind of tool that perhaps the only way to describe them is to give their uses. As their names suggest, they are used for cutting out brushwood and trimming hedges. The long-handled kind is probably the most useful because it allows you to use your strength most efficiently. When you use it, strike down and across the sapling, rather than straight across.

A word about safety. Brushing hooks and the like are closely related to halberds and battle-axes and they are just as dangerous in the wrong hands. If you have any doubts about your ability to use them safely, use long handled loppers or a saw instead. They are slower, but they leave you with all your fingers and toes.

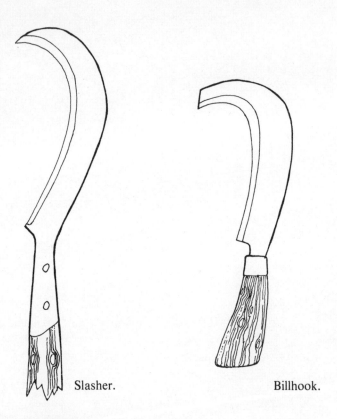

Slasher.   Billhook.

Pruners and Loppers
Pruners are used with one hand for the light trimming and shaping of fruit trees and shrubs. Loppers, which have two long handles and work in the same way, will cut branches up to one inch thick. Forestry workers sometimes use loppers with extra-long handles and gigantic cutting jaws. These will cope with woods two inches thick. For high branches, you need what is called a 'tree-lopper' which is nothing more than a long pole with pruners on the end.

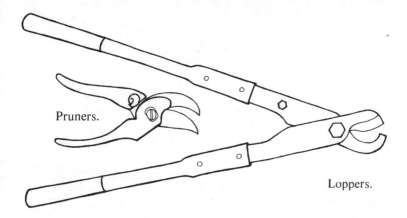

Pruners.

Loppers.

Hedge Clippers
You will only need these when your garden is in order. They are not intended for heavy work and you should not try to cut anything over a quarter of an inch thick with them.

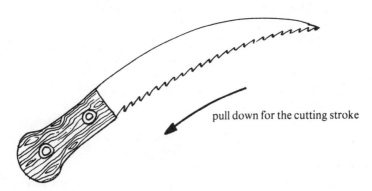

pull down for the cutting stroke

Curved pruning saw.

Saws
Pruning saws will lop branches up to four inches thick. The best kind has backward-pointing teeth and an incurved blade. This means that the saw cuts on the pull-stroke, which is very useful when cutting

above one's head. For thicker branches a log saw is the answer.

POWER TOOLS

Small Petrol Engines

The first thing to remember about small petrol engines is that they are intended to go – and go on going – for hours and, if necessary, for days on end. Things can go wrong with them but generally a modern engine can be started and kept running by anyone. So don't be frightened of them. The second thing to remember is that they may be small but they are also extremely powerful. A buzzing little three horse-power engine will not stop if you put your finger in the way of the flywheel. It will not pause for a moment, it will take your finger off. So, treat engines with respect, please.

If you hire a machine with an engine, it is a good idea to get the man in the shop to show you the layout of the engine and how to start it, and how to stop it.

Small petrol engines are divided into two types which, for our purposes, differ in the sort of fuel they use and how they are lubricated.

Two-strokes

These are most often found on smaller or older mowing machines. They use a special fuel, a mixture of petrol and oil, most usually in the proportion of half a pint of oil to a gallon of petrol. They have no sump, no dipstick – the oil in the fuel lubricates the engine as it goes. Ask the man at the garage to mix the fuel for you if you are in doubt. If you have to mix it yourself, do not use one of the modern 20-50 oils as the detergents in these can be harmful to the engine. Use an S.A.E. 30 oil, which is cheaper anyway. Some manufacturers of two-strokes produce their own oils for mixing with petrol. These are often sold in small sachets of the exact quantity you need.

I must emphasize that if you try to run a two-stroke engine on ordinary petrol, it will seize up almost at once, and the engine could be ruined.

Four-strokes

These are like the engine in your car. They use straight petrol – two-star is good enough. They are lubricated with the same sort of oil that you have in your car engine, and you are much more likely to encounter this type than a two-stroke. In general, they are quieter, vibrate less and start and re-start more easily.

How to Start a Small Engine
Engines differ, of course, so the following points are suggested as guidelines only. I don't pretend that everything that can be known is given here:
1. Make sure that you have the right kind of fuel in the tank and turn on the fuel tap which is usually found directly underneath it.
2. If you have a four-stroke, ensure that the sump is filled with oil to the correct level.
3. Put on the choke fully. This gives the engine what is called a 'rich' mixture to start on. You will find the choke lever on the carburettor. It will probably be marked 'on' and 'off'.
4. Prime the carburettor, which is the device that mixes the petrol with air before it passes into the engine. You prime it, that is fill it up, by repeatedly pressing a little button on the top until fuel overflows. On some engines, this may not be necessary.
5. Open the throttle lever fully. This is generally good advice but you may have to experiment to find the best setting.
6. Make sure that the business-end of the machine, the rotors or whatever, is disengaged from the engine.
7. Make sure that the 'stop' switch is not depressed.
8. The engine is now ready to go. Starting devices are many and varied but the most common involves pulling a cord wrapped round the pulley of the flywheel. Give one easy pull to get the feel of the mechanism and then try again, much harder. Keep trying. With some engines you have to use a lot of muscle. Once the engine starts, gradually close the throttle and open the choke until it is ticking over. Let the engine warm up for a minute or two before starting heavy work. On a cold day an engine may stall if it is made to try too hard all at once.

What to Do if it Doesn't Start
First of all go through the starting drill given above and make sure that you have missed nothing. If you haven't, ask yourself the following questions:

1. Is there fuel?
2. Is the fuel getting to the engine? Check again with the priming-button.
3. Is the fuel clean? Clean the fuel-filter which will be between the tank and the carburettor. Do not be frightened of doing this. They are usually very simple devices.
4. Is there a spark? Take off the sparkplug with a plug-spanner or ring spanner of the appropriate size. With the plug still connected to its electrical lead, hold it (by its ceramic insulation or the lead) against the cylinder head and pull the starting handle. This will be easy because there is no compression with the plug out. If all is well, you should see a vigorous little blue spark. Do this in a shady corner so that the spark can be more easily seen. If there is no spark, take the plug off and clean it with fine emery-paper or scratch it clean with the blade of your knife. Check the gap between the electrodes. You will need a set of feeler-gauges for this. Plugs differ, but 0.25 of an inch is common. If the gap is too narrow, the electricity will cross it without making a spark at all; if it is too wide it won't have the energy for so vast a leap. No spark yet? Get a plug off another machine that you know works and try that. Still no joy? Then the trouble is probably the magneto where the current is generated and for that you will need to call in an expert.
5. Is the engine flooded? This means that the cylinder-head and plug are so saturated with fuel that ignition cannot take place. Take out the plug. If it is wet then the engine is flooded. Leave off the plug (clean it, of course) and open the choke fully for half an hour to let the excess fuel evaporate. Then try again, using less choke and throttle. If the engine still floods, even with minimum settings, the carburettor needs adjusting and for this you will have to call in a mechanic. Unless you have done it yourself successfully and know a great deal about it, don't try to take the carburettor to pieces.

Assuming you have been through all these checks and the machine still won't start, you have a problem. It may be any of a dozen things, all of which are best left to a mechanic.

Small Diesel Engines
You are unlikely to encounter these except on certain makes of very

TOOLS AND HOW TO USE THEM

large rotavator. They are usually noisier than a petrol engine but they have much to be said for them – they pull well, use cheaper fuel and have no electrical system to go wrong – no plug, no magneto, no nothing.

Starting them is easy. There is a handle on the flywheel that you turn round and round. Once you have the flywheel revolving fairly briskly, you flip over the compression-lever, which is on top of the cylinder. This has the effect of suddenly increasing the pressure within the cylinder so that the diesel fuel ignites without the need for a spark.

Emergency Stops
There is a situation, beloved of cartoonists, in which a lawnmower, out of control and dragging a helpless gardener, hurtles through hedges and glasshouses, smashing and rending as it goes. But it is not so funny when it happens to you.

Of course, most engines are fitted with stop-devices which rarely fail. If they do, however, you may have to act quickly. Turning off the petrol doesn't stop an engine at once; you must cut off the electrical current to the sparking plug. Rip off the lead. If it is permanently attached (some are screwed down) you will have to short-circuit the system. Do this by making a bridge with a screwdriver, or the blade of spade or trowel, between the spark plug and the cylinder head. This will carry the current to earth. When you make this bridge, put your screwdriver on the cylinder-head first and not on the plug, otherwise you will get a nasty jolt up your arm. If all else fails and the machine is moving, tip it over; throw it off its wheels. Watch out for yourself when you do this, for the engine may not stop at once and the handlebars and rotors may start to revolve, instead of the wheel.

Rotavators
There are three basic types, only two of which need concern us here. First of all, there is the sort with powered wheels. This is undoubtedly the easiest for the inexperienced to use. The wheels pull the machine along while rotating tines break up the ground. In the second type, both cultivation and traction are provided by the tines. This type requires more knack to handle and at first a good deal of muscle, especially in the shoulders and back.

For breaking new ground, the heavier the machine the better. Go over your patch before you start to see that there are no bricks or large stones left which could shatter the tines. Make sure that there is no old fencing wire or binder twine left lying to entangle the blades. Let the machine take its time and gradually work down to its full depth of cultivation.

There is not much to choose between the two types in terms of cultivating efficiency. The wheelless type is easier to transport if you hire it. Generally the handles fold and the rotors can be removed.

Some machines have a reverse gear, which is handy when turning. Never, never leave the rotors in gear when you are reversing. If you stumble and fall (as you are quite likely to do, since you are walking backwards) the rotavator won't stop, it will chew you up and spit you out again.

Mowing Machines
There are two types to consider, the rotary and the sort with blades like a series of gigantic scissors. The 'scissors' type is sometimes referred to as a powered scythe. Old makes have large wheels and can be rather difficult to handle. Newer models have much smaller wheels and are lighter altogether. One, called a 'scrub-cutter' has a tiny two-stroke motor and is carried slung from the shoulder by a length of webbing. All these machines will cut grass and heavy weeds up to five or six feet high.

Rotary machines are nothing more than larger and more powerful versions of the machines that many people already use for their lawns. To cut rank growth they have to be pushed very slowly. I do not think they are absolutely suitable for clearing grass and weeds off neglected ground. But if you do use one, make sure there are no stones left lying. If the blades of the mower strike a stone, it will take off at a quite startling velocity and such a missile could easily put out someone's eye.

Power Saws
I cannot recommend the use of a power saw (or chain saw, as they are sometimes called) to anyone who has not been properly trained in their use. If you positively must make use of one, say, to fell a number of trees or any tree over fifteen feet high, call in an expert forester or tree-surgeon. Even such a relatively small tree can do an awful lot of damage if it falls the wrong way.

TOOLS AND HOW TO USE THEM

Hedge-trimmers, Electrical and Petrol-powered
Don't consider these unless you have more than 50 yards of hedge to look after and very little time. Otherwise they are not worth the expense. However, for taming a much-overgrown hedge, a petrol driven machine is a good idea. Take care of your fingers.

Flameguns
These are nothing more than very large paraffin blow-lamps and they work in exactly the same way as a blow-lamp. So long as they are treated with respect they are quite safe to use and quite effective as well. The bigger sort is usually mounted on wheels and is rather less handy than the hand-held type. Lighting them is simple. Having cleaned the nozzle, (for which a tool is provided) and filled the tank, you shut the valve and give the pressurizing pump two or three strokes. Open the valve a little and let through just enough paraffin to soak the asbestos-cloth wick below the nozzle. Turn off the valve and light the wick. After about three minutes the nozzle should begin to put out a hard tongue of flame accompanied by a harsh roaring noise. At this point, turn on the valve slowly and give a few more strokes on the pump. Do this gradually, until the gun is burning with a steady roar, and the pressure-gauge shows 25 p.s.i. If the nozzle starts spitting out unvapourized paraffin, which burns with black smoke as it goes, it means the coils around the nozzle have not been heated enough. Turn off the valve and wait a few seconds before starting again. Once you have the gun going, try not to stop until the tank is empty. It is rather like a car; it takes far more fuel to set it in motion than to keep it going.

Don't try to burn all the vegetation to ashes in one go. Aim the tongue of flame at the base of the weeds until they flop over, then wait a few days until they have died and browned and go over them again. It is a smoky job best done in warm weather, but watch out for little running fires.

An obvious point about safety: don't try to run a flamegun on petrol. You will end up in little charred pieces if you do.

The great drawback to using a flamegun is that it destroys organic matter and hence humus. On the other hand, it will kill weed seeds and in a neglected garden, where weeds will probably be the number one problem for several years, this is a great advantage. A flamegun will kill annual weeds outright but not deep-rooted perennials, such as docks and dandelions, which will soon put out fresh leaves. However, it will keep such weeds from growing and seeding until you get round to digging them out.

Measuring Tools
A measuring stick and a garden line are things you can make yourself quite easily. They are essential even from the first day, if only for you to see what you are up against. Your stick should be six feet or two metres long, marked with saw-cuts every 10cm or three inches. Use synthetic orange string for your line. It is tough, won't rot and you can see it easily.

Improvising and Making Your Own
This has been a long and I hope exhaustive chapter, but I don't want to leave you with the impression that you must have every tool I have mentioned and that they must all be bought new. Of course, you haven't and they needn't. They can be borrowed, bought second-hand and some of them you can make yourself. Farm and auction sales are a good source of second-hand tools, farm-sales especially. At these, hand tools tend not to be much regarded and are often sold off in bundles very cheaply. Don't worry, if you bid, that you may be getting a bundle of unrecognizable wood and steel along with the muck fork you covet. The other items will come in handy one day, you may be sure.

If you have the time, you can make tools yourself and you do not have to be a mechanical genius to do it. At one time, nearly all tools used in the countryside were made by the local blacksmith with very unsophisticated equipment. Your local secondary school has just such equipment in its metalwork shop, and you can get the chance to use it at evening classes. These are cheap and very informal, and the metalwork teacher will be there to give you friendly advice. He may even do the difficult bits for you, just for the pleasure of showing off. I have recently made myself hoes, rakes and trowels at classes like these. Even such a relatively complex item as a barrow is not beyond the scope of an amateur. I know, because I have just made one myself out of the frame of an old bed, corrugated-iron roofing beaten flat and the discarded wheel and tyre of a B.M.C. 1100. I don't like to boast, but it is magnificent and cost not more than £2 for nuts, bolts and paint.

4
SETTING TO WORK

Before you lay a hand on a tool you must make a plan. This involves a certain amount of long-term thinking, answering such questions as 'what do I want a garden for?' and, 'will I be able to maintain it?' But having answered these kind of questions, there are other shorter-term priorities that need to be decided upon. I have listed and discussed them below. They are in rough order of urgency. You may find, in your garden, that other things need to be done first. I offer them as guidelines only.

1. Destroy the weeds.
2. Mark out the plots and paths.
3. Get rid of the rubbish.
4. Break the ground.
5. See to the drainage.
6. Rescue operations.
7. Take a picture for posterity.

DESTROY THE WEEDS

Or at the very least, prevent them from seeding. In a neglected garden, rather than a new one, weeds are the number one problem. It is an awful thing to go into a garden for the first time and find the weeds six feet high and scattering their seeds by the million.

You may know the old saying, 'one year of seed, seven years of weed.' It is no exaggeration: if anything, it understates the case. The plants we call weeds are amongst the most successful and well-adapted in all nature. They are successful plants because they are tough, grow quickly, adapt to a very wide range of soil and climatic conditions and propagate themselves in a wide variety of ways. The sow thistle, for instance, has deep-travelling white roots, which, if disturbed by digging, break up easily into small pieces, any of which is capable of making a new plant. When the sow thistle flowers, it produces seed rather like that of a dandelion. It blows far and wide. Other weeds, like groundsel, produce seed which germinates at intervals. Some may grow into little weeds at once, others may wait like little time-bombs for up to ten years before bursting into life to plague the gardener. Groundsel and chickweed will start into growth again if lifted with their roots intact and left lying on the ground, instead of being taken away.

So weeds are tough customers. Kill them. Suffer not one to live, still less reproduce itself.

If you have a strong flush of weeds, take them down at once with a scythe, or whatever tool you prefer. It will make the job of cultivation much easier if you try and trim them as close to the ground as you can. Having taken off the heavy growth with a scythe, you could perhaps follow it with a rotary mower. If you can borrow a goat for a few days, she will do a very good job for you. The owner will be pleased to have some free grazing – but make sure that nanny is securely tethered. Goats are extremely intelligent, agile beasts and if they can escape and eat something they shouldn't, they will.

Once you have the top-growth clipped close, you can cultivate by whatever method you favour. Before you do so, however, I suggest you get hold of a flamegun and go over the ground with it a few times. This is a nasty, smoky job but one which will pay dividends by destroying weed-seeds.

This suggestion will, I know, offend some committed organic gardeners because the flamegun will also destroy much humus and many organisms living on or near the soil surface. You will have to balance the equation between this ecological loss and reducing the crop of weeds in future years.

Compost Heap or Bonfire?
If the weeds are large, mature and producing seed, I don't think you have much choice; you must burn them. Skilled and experienced composters, who can build a heap and guarantee that it will heat up to 170°F (75°C) and thereby kill all the weed seeds, can ignore this advice. But if you have never built a compost heap before, burn the weeds and avoid trouble.

On the other hand, if you catch them early, before they have formed seed and while they are young and sappy, by all means, compost them.

How to Build a Compost Heap

Composting is not an art, it is a science – that is, if you follow the rules and understand what you are about, you will make good compost. The first thing to aim for, in building a heap, is high temperature. A hot heap means that the fungi and bacteria are hard at work breaking down the vegetable and kitchen wastes and cooking the weed seeds. If you are very interested, you can buy a hot-bed thermometer, which is nothing more than an ordinary long thermometer enclosed in a pointed alloy tube, which will tell you if the heap is reaching the desired temperature. To attain and keep up this temperature, the heap will need to be of reasonable size. Heaps smaller than a cubic metre tend not to heat up reliably.

For the smaller quantities of waste, use a bin. You can buy bins but none I've seen are any better than one you could make yourself. The best system is to have two bins, side by side, so that while one is heating and maturing, the other is being filled up.

You can make bins out of all sorts of materials, providing you bear the following points in mind: the sides must insulate the compost and prevent loss of heat; the top of the bin must be insulated for the same reason; there must be provision underneath the bin for the entry of air; and the whole structure should be roofed to keep out the chilling rain.

Put into more practical terms this means that you can build the sides of the bin from bricks, blocks or old packing cases. Some composters say that the sides of the bin should be pierced at intervals to allow the entry of air but recent research suggests that if plenty of air is allowed to enter the bottom of the heap, this is sufficient. You can make a good bin with straw bales. They are easy to handle, will last a couple of seasons and can in the end be composted themselves. The front of the bins should be removable if possible. This makes filling and emptying very much easier.

You can let air into the heap by laying a few land or drainage tiles at the bottom. A layer of brushwood or prunings will do as well. A few old blankets, or a layer of collapsed cardboard boxes will do to insulate the top of the heap. Corrugated iron will roof it or polythene will do, if it is stretched tight to allow the rain to run off.

If you have a great deal of material to compost, it may not be practical to put it into bins. You must build a heap. It ought not to be more than six feet (two metres) high, or wide. It can be of indefinite length. As with a bin, try and insulate the heap if you can. Some people simply cover the whole thing with a big sheet of black polythene. This practice seems to break all the rules about letting plenty of air pass through the heap, but it does work.

When it comes to the building of the heap, or the filling of the bin, the best way is to gather and mix all the materials separately and then put them in all at once. This enables the rotting process to get off to a flying start.

Activators
The organisms that perform the composting process need food in the form of nitrogen. If you can get hold of manure, mix it with the wastes before you build the heap. Any sort of manure will do, the fresher the better. Fish meal and blood and bone meal are good sources of nitrogen, although they are expensive. You can also buy herbal activators, which work.

My own practice is cheap, rather disgusting and never fails. I use my own urine. I keep a bucket in the coal shed which fills surprisingly quickly. My two small sons are very willing helpers. When I have built a heap, I dilute two gallons of urine at about four to one and pour it over the top. The smell vanishes in a day or so.

Compost Materials
Anything that was once alive can be composted. This includes any kitchen waste, stale bread, chicken carcases, mattress stuffing, old wool and cotton clothes. Very woody materials, like brussels sprout stems, should be chopped up. Plastics and metals won't rot. Oddly enough, cheese is very resistant as well. Nettles are a wonderful material. They seem to provide plenty of heat.

Siting the Heap
If possible, place the heap or bin on broken cultivated ground. This will enable worms to enter the heap from underneath and complete the process of decomposition. It is a sign of maturity in compost when it

contains a lot of worms.

Building the Heap

Assuming you have mixed all the materials previously, all you have to do – if you are using a bin – is throw it in, trampling it at intervals. Throw in a few handfuls of earth, lime or bonfire ash at the same time. The lime stops the heap from becoming too acid, thereby holding up the process of decomposition. The ashes or earth absorb ammonia (from the activator) until the bacteria can make use of it. If you are building a heap, try to keep the sides as vertical as you can, lay the wastes in a ring around the outside. The centre of the heap will almost fill up by itself. If you start building from the centre, you will end up with a conical heap, which will not retain heat as well as a square-sided heap.

The compost should reach its maximum temperature in about a week. Thereafter it cools and the compost should be mature after two or three months. It should be brown and crumbly. If it's wet and smelly, something has gone wrong. Compost heaps most usually go wrong when they are built too slowly, so that the rotting process never really gets started, or if the materials are not well mixed. For instance, a thick layer of grass clippings will soon rot into a thick, slimy mass which effectively prevents air reaching the rest of the heap. Don't expect too much of a heap built in the autumn or winter. The best time of year for composting is from spring through to late summer. Plenty of material is usually available and the warmer air permits and assists rapid decomposition.

MARK OUT THE PLOTS AND PATHS

Do this carefully, with a measuring stick and line. Use rows of stick to mark out the outlines. If you are planning a flower-bed with a curved edge, lay out a hose to mark the shapes. Rows of sticks and bits of hose left lying about may look pretty silly and don't in themselves make a garden, but they help you to keep the object of all your sweat and trouble firmly in view.

There are many excellent books about garden planning and I suggest you read as many of them as possible. As a practical point, allow enough space in your plan for a good hard path running along the main axis of your vegetable plot. It should be no less than three feet (one metre) wide. This will save you scratching your knuckles on plants and posts as you push your barrow down it.

GET RID OF THE RUBBISH

The first thing to decide is what exactly constitutes rubbish. If yours is a new house the builders will no doubt have left behind all sorts of stuff. You can find a use for a surprising amount of it, as I hope the following list will prove.

Bricks and blocks. As valuable as gold and twice as useful. Even half-bricks have their uses. They save you cutting up whole ones. Spare bricks can be made to occupy much less space if you stack them carefully.

Timber. Never throw it away, even if it seems only fit for firewood. You'll find out how valuable it is when you actually come to try and buy the stuff.

Rubble. This includes small pieces of broken brick, spare hard core and the like. Keep it for the foundations of paths.

Sand and gravel. Builders' sand is usually too fine to be of any use in potting composts but you can bed small paving stones and bricks on it. If you have children, make them a sandpit with all those bricks and blocks and pieces of quite useless timber. I don't see a builder leaving behind enough gravel to surface any length of path but small quantities will come in handy for improving the drainage in planting holes.

Plaster board and hydrated lime. Some old-fashioned builders may leave you some lime. Keep it to apply to the garden (see Chapter Two for specific advice). Plaster board is made of gypsum, which is the best form of lime for breaking up clay.

Drain pipes. Depending on the width and length of the pipe, these can be used for blanching celery and forcing sea kale and rhubarb.

BREAKING THE GROUND

All the best authorities say that digging should be completed by Christmas – and rightly so. Soil, especially heavy soil, benefits from exposure to wind, rain and frost. Frost in particular. After the turn of the year, the weather always seems to get wetter and cultivation correspondingly more difficult. Trying to dig sodden ground is a futile process. It will break your back and your heart, as well as doing great damage to the structure of the soil. So if you have missed the ideal pre-Christmas period, don't panic. Wait until the winds of March have dried out the soil. You will have to hurry then, but it can be done. However, if you have a large plot, it will be a good idea to cultivate only a part of it and really look after the crops you grow there, rather than do a rush job on the whole plot and end up at the end of the season with miserable crops choked with weeds. If you do this, remember to keep the weeds on the uncultivated patch in check with a mower or a scythe.

Digging

If you are faced with only a flush of weeds, perhaps on cultivated ground that has been neglected for only a season, it may be sufficient to single dig your plot. Mark out your ground, as suggested in the diagram below – that is, divide it into two longitudinal strips. Take out a trench to the width and depth of your spade at the head of strip 'A' and throw it in a heap beyond the head of strip 'B'. Now dig your way down the strip in the direction of the arrows. When you get to the foot of strip 'A', you will find yourself left with a trench. Fill this with the soil you dig from a trench across the foot of strip 'B' and then dig your way back up to the head of the strip. When you get there, you will find yourself with a trench to fill in. Do it with the soil you dug from the very first trench in strip 'A', which will be conveniently at hand.

As you dig, try to throw the soil slightly away from you, leaving a clear trench. You can throw muck in this trench if you have any. Hold the spade as nearly upright as you can. Take your time to get used to the work and don't try to take too big a slice with the spade. Four inches (10cm) is big enough at first.

As you go on, remove as many roots of perennial weeds as you can. This interrupts the rhythm of your work but it is obviously worthwhile in the long run. Before you dig a row, skim the weeds off the ground you intend to dig and throw them in the bottom of the clear trench you have made. Ten inches down, most of them will do no more harm and will add humus to the soil as they rot. While you are doing this, it's worth remembering that weeds aren't all bad. Someone once called them 'the guardians of the soil', and this is quite true. A flush of weeds, while it can be a great nuisance, is covering the soil surface and preventing erosion and the breakdown of soil structure as well as fixing nutrients which will be released when they rot.

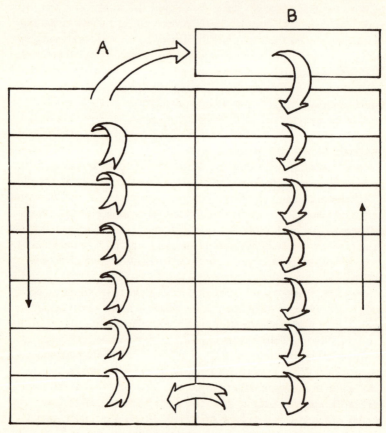

Single digging routine.

You may be lucky and have a new house built on old pasture land. This is very likely to be wonderful soil. There is nothing like growing grass for building up fertility. However, in these circumstances, single digging is not enough. You must skim off the turf and stack it, leaving the bare earth to be single dug. Take the thinnest slice you can when you remove the turf (you might be able to borrow the ideal tool, a turfing iron, for this job.) Stack the turf carefully, grass down, in a rectangular heap. When the stack is finished, cover it with a sheet of black polythene, which will prevent the grass growing again. You can pierce the sheet and plant marrows or pumpkins through the holes: they'll do wonderfully well. After a year, remove the sheet and you will have a heap of wonderful loam, ideal for making potting compost for tomatoes and chrysanthemums.

Double Digging

If you feel the need to cultivate your ground deeply, you can double dig it. This is an old-established practice but recent comparative tests have shown that it makes little difference to the performance of crops. However, on new ground, it may be the only method available to the amateur of removing deep-rooted weeds and breaking up the subsoil. Think of it as a once and for all effort. An important point: when double-digging, never invert the layers of soil; leave the subsoil underneath and the top soil on top. You can cultivate grassland this way but it must be clean land, with no couch in it. Rough, dirty grassland is best broken by stripping the turf. Burying couch is buying endless trouble.

Start double-digging by marking out the plot as for single-digging, into two strips. Take out a trench (see diagram) at the head of strip 'C' to the depth of your spade, but two spade-widths wide. Put the soil at the head of strip 'D'. If you're digging grassland, put the stripped turf in a separate heap. Break up, but do not invert, the soil at the bottom of the trench. Now move backwards down strip 'C' and mark out a second trench the same width as the first. Strip off the turf and throw it, grass downwards into the bottom of your first trench, followed by the rest of the soil from the second trench. If you are digging already-cultivated ground in this way, you can incorporate muck into the second spit (that is, the bottom of the trench) as you go. Dig your way to the bottom of strip 'C' then proceed much as for single digging, that is, fill up the last trench in strip 'C' with the sods and earth from strip 'D'. Work your way back up to the head of the plot and fill in your last trench with the heap you will find waiting there.

As you will have gathered, double-digging is very hard, tedious work. You should only undertake if you are absolutely convinced that it's going to do a lot of good.

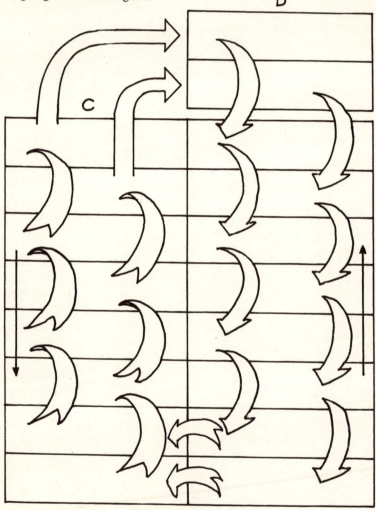

Double digging routine.

Machine Cultivation

I have described rotavators and their uses in the chapter about tools so I shall make only a few additional points and repeat this one: make sure that the top-growth is as short as you can make it and go over the ground meticulously for large stones, wire and anything else likely to hinder the rotors. It's a good idea to go over the ground, prodding it with a fork. In my own new garden it would have been fatal to have rotavated it without doing this first. Beneath the matted surface growth and a skim of earth I discovered the foundations of a greenhouse, a disused septic tank and a flagged path, all of which would have instantly destroyed the rotors of any machine driven across them.

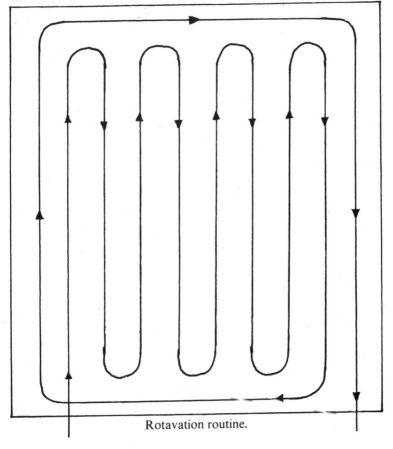

Rotavation routine.

Be as methodical about rotavation as you would be about digging. I suggest you follow the plan in the following diagram. Cultivate the length of the plot first and finish off by making a few passes across the headlands.

It will take a few sessions with a rotavator to break down grassland adequately and even then you may have to spend some time with a fork and a rake before you get an adequate tilth. There are always a few obdurate sods that resist. You may have to rake these up and remove them altogether.

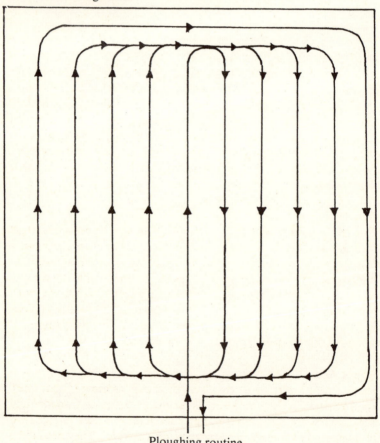

Ploughing routine.

SETTING TO WORK

Some of the larger rotavators will pull a single-bladed plough. Ploughs usually cut and throw the sod to the right, so that you cannot quite follow the same pattern of cultivation as you would for a rotavator. Start in the centre of your plot and work you way outwards, furrow by furrow, doing the headlands last of all.

Follow the plough with a rotavator. Autumn-turned ground may only need a few passes with a harrow attachment.

One Method Not to Use

There is one method used for breaking new ground that you will often see practised, but I cannot recommend it. It is the way which seems most obvious to new gardeners and it consists of digging over the turf or weeds with a fork, shaking off the soil and carting them away. Don't do it. It is tedious, frustrating, time-wasting and inefficient. If the top-growth is weedy, get rid of it. Skim it off, burn it and leave the ground as bare as you can. Then, dig out and get rid of the weed roots or punish them repeatedly with a rotavator. If the top growth is clean turf, you don't have to worry, just dig it in somehow. There is no point in pretending that making a new garden or rescuing a neglected one is anything other than hard work. Use your head, the most intelligent method you can and leave your enthusiasm unblunted for the more pleasant aspects of gardening.

Tractors

On a really big plot of over two acres it will be worth your while to get a tractor, not only to make the initial cultivations but subsequent ones as well. If you just want to hire a man and his machine to break the ground, make sure he can get in and out and that he can turn easily within the confines of your garden. Don't forget to make the same tests for obstructions in the soil as you would for a rotavator. Check the position of the house drains. Even a little 'Fergie' is quite heavy enough to shatter these if they are too close to the surface.

Animal Assistants

I have already referred to goats and their uses as mowing machines. Another beast likely to be useful is the pig. Pigs dig, and wonderfully efficient they are too. However, you cannot allow a pair of pigs (two for company) to wander just anywhere on your plot. They need to be fenced so that they can concentrate their efforts. They also need to be fed. Pigs are wonderfully omnivorous. If you can get hold of swill, so much the better but you must boil it, otherwise you risk spreading disease. You can buy pig feed by the bag. In country districts, all sorts of people keep pigs at the ends of their gardens, so you can always find someone to give you advice.

In a surburban situation, you will have to ask your district health office about regulations concerning pigs. Don't go ahead and get the beasts and then wait for someone to object: someone always will. There are all sorts of people who imagine that pigs must stink just because they are pigs. You would stink if you lived in a cramped shed that no-one ever cleaned out. Kept in a civilized manner, in the open, with space to move about, pigs stink no more than horses and cows.

Hens have their uses as well. If they're kept fenced, their scratching will soon clear a patch of ground for you. Throw in household wastes, straw and shavings for them to rake through. After a few months, move them to another patch and either remove the material left to the compost heap (this is a very good way of mixing wastes) or dig it in.

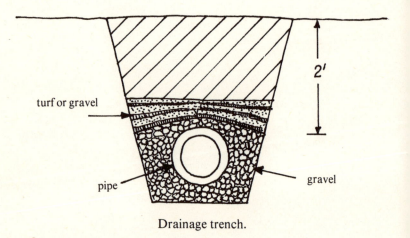

Drainage trench.

SEE TO THE DRAINAGE

I have mentioned this topic briefly in Chapter Two. Unless your plot is an obvious swamp, wait a bit and try ordinary cultivation before setting out to drain it. Breaking the ground and leaving the soil in large, rough clods exposes a large area to sun and wind so that a great deal of moisture can be evaporated. Double digging may break up the subsoil just enough to let the excess water drain away. There may be drains already in the ground. The outlet into a main ditch may be blocked; if so, find it and unblock it. A simple thing like that may have an enormous effect.

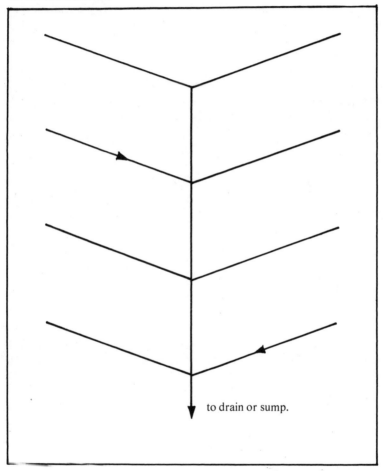

Drainage ditch pattern.

However, if you decide there is nothing else for it but to drain, ask advice first. If you have a plot large enough to be called a smallholding the Agricultural Development and Advisory Service may help. Otherwise you must depend on the goodwill and advice of neighbouring farmes and gardeners.

Drains are passages made through the soil, beyond the usual depth of cultivation, that allow excess water to flow away. You can make drains with land tiles, which are porous earthenware pipes laid end to end in the soil down to a main drain or ditch, or you can make your own with flat stones laid on bricks or even bundles of brushwood. The latter can survive a surprisingly long time.

Dig trenches, two feet deep, in a herring-bone pattern. The frequency of the trenches depends very much on how wet the soil is. Obviously, the wetter the soil the closer the ribs of the herring have to be. About 10 to 25 feet (3-5m) is an average distance. Lay in your tiles or whatever cheaper alternative you choose on a layer of gravel and cover them with turf, grass-side down, which is cheaper than another layer of gravel. The turf or gravel are designed to prevent silt and clay from being washed into the pipes and eventually blocking them. Make sure that all your trenches have an adequate fall: the greater the fall, the less likely the system is to clog. You can test this by the simple method of throwing buckets of water, first down the trenches as you dig them and then down the finished system. Remember that all the water draining from your land must go into a drain, or a ditch or a sump. You can't just let it flow on to someone else's field or garden.
drain, or a ditch or a sump. You can't just let it flow on to someone else's field or garden.

If there isn't a drain or ditch, you will have to build a sump. This is simply a hole, at least one metre square. The bottom should be at least 18 inches (50cm) below the last pipe leading into it. Fill the hole with rubble and mark its position in some permanent way. All drainage systems clog in the end and one day you'll have to heave out all the rubble to try and clear away all the silt that will have accumulated in the bottom. If your poor drainage is caused by a layer of impermeable soil, then the bottom of your sump must be below it. On a smaller patch a sump by itself may provide adequate drainage.

Another simple system is to dig what is called an interception ditch. It may be that your poor drainage stems from water seeping into your plot from the land above it. Dig a good deep ditch across the high side of your garden and then away down one side. Once more, make sure there is somewhere for the water to go.

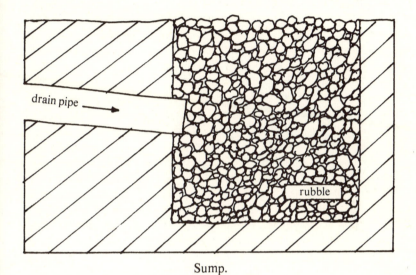

Sump.

RESCUE OPERATIONS

Lawns

You can usually tell where the lawn used to be in a neglected garden: the grass, even though it may be three feet tall, still has an homogeneous look to it. If what you decide used to be the lawn has brambles and six foot thistles growing in it, it may be best to clear and cultivate the area and start again. Otherwise, do the obvious thing and cut it. Keep cutting it, rake it with a spring-tined rake, spike it with a fork or a patent lawn aerator. Cutting encourages new growth; raking gets rid of the old yellow grass (of which there is a surprising amount in a supposedly well-kept lawn) and spiking breaks up the compacted surface and lets air down to the roots. Treated thus, a lawn will recover, not to bowling-green standard, but to something tolerably green and smooth, over a couple of seasons.

Herbaceous Borders

Old borders infested with perennial weeds can be a great problem. You can work away with a hoe and fork and clean much of it but the couch grass and the ground elder will still be hiding amongst the roots of peonies and Michaelmas daisies and every spring they will creep out and try to colonize the ground you have so carefully cleared.

insert forks back to back and push handles together.

Division of plants.

Probably the best solution is to get to work in the dormant season of the year (October to March), lift all the plants and heel them in elsewhere. Then cultivate the border thoroughly, dig and dig until all the weeds are out. To be really safe, muck it well and grow potatoes. The constant cultivation that potatoes need will put an end to any remaining weeds. When you lift the potatoes be sure you leave no little ones in the ground. They are quite a nasty weed in themselves and not at all easy to eradicate.

Meanwhile, sort out the plants that you have heeled in. Most herbaceous plants can be divided in one way or another and are all the better for it. You get more plants this way and by choosing the outer growth of a plant you will have more vigorous ones as well. For example, plants like Michaelmas daisies and hardy geraniums can be divided with two forks set back to back, as in the illustration.

Some plants, notably old lupins, will not survive lifting. You will simply have to accept a few casualties. Most plants can be replaced – lupins for instance can easily be raised from seed. I suggest you consult a good book about herbaceous borders (see the book-list at the end of this book.)

Shrubs

It is more difficult to give advice in this case than for herbaceous borders. Shrubs can be so big and so well-established that simply moving them is out of the question. Some shrubs, like rhododendrons and some conifers, have compact furry root-balls, so that they can be moved with surprising ease. But even then, you will not be able to remove the concealed weed roots. Most are best left exactly where they are.

The first step is to prune, and prune correctly. Consult the most compendious book you can about this. Shrubs differ considerably in their pruning needs. However, as a brief guide, remember that shrubs are pruned for the following reasons:
1. To remove dead and diseased wood.
2. To remove crossing or rubbing wood.
3. To remove dead flowers.
4. To promote fresh growth.
5. To shape and give space to surrounding plants.

After pruning, take a fresh look at the border and decide if it's overcrowded, even if you like all the plants in it. If you happen not to like azaleas, don't be put off by the fact that everyone else does: have them out and grow something you do like.

Finally, get in there after the weeds. Well-grown shrubs provide a dense leaf-cover that intercepts the light and makes it very hard for weeds to grow underneath. A mulch of peat or compost will take care of annual weeds; your fork and a measure of persistence will take care of the rest.

Hedges

With hedges, as with lawns, you do the obvious thing: you cut them. Not all at once, but gradually, so that after a season or two, you have a hedge of the dimensions you want. Hedging plants are selected because they will stand cutting, so don't be afraid that you might kill them. However, as always, there is an exception and that is lavender. If you cut lavender back further than the previous two year's growth it will probably die.

Fruit

The test here is, is it worth it? Diseased and senile trees and bushes are simply not worth preserving. Buy healthy young stock and avoid trouble. This is particularly true of soft fruit. Strawberries can fruit the year after planting and none of the others take more than three years to come into bearing. It is easy nowadays to buy stock that is called 'Ministry Certified'. This means that the stock plants have been inspected in the nursery by officials from the Ministry of Agriculture and are guaranteed to be free of certain virus diseases. Always buy such stock if you can.

With top fruit – apples, plums, pears and so on – the story is rather different. Newly planted top fruit takes more than just a few years to come into full bearing, so it may be worthwhile to try and rescue trees which are perhaps suffering from some nutritional deficiency, which can be corrected by correct manuring, or the effects of bad pruning or no pruning at all. Old farm gardens always seem to have a few old apple trees which could be brought back into productive life by the judicious use of pruners and saw.

Beyond saying that it may be worthwhile, I shall not try to give specific advice about the job. Very much fatter books than this have been written about the management of fruit trees and you should consult as many as you can before picking up the pruners (see the reading list).

And, of course, there is always someone who knows about these things who can look at your trees and say exactly what needs to be done.

Paths and Drives

Unless they are very solid concrete, all paths and drives tend to deteriorate sooner or later. And even concrete can be destroyed once frost has cracked the surface a little, the rain has washed in a little dust for soil and the wind has carried a weed seed to germinate and grow in it. Asphalt goes the same way, only quicker. Nothing illustrates the power of a growing plant more vividly than to see little spears of couch grass sticking up through asphalt or to see whole sections of it lifted cleanly up by a buried daffodil bulb pushing for the light. These problems are much magnified in the case of gravel or paving paths. These give the microscopic wind-born seed every chance – and they usually take it.

Gravel paths and drives are by far the worst. If you have one already you will know that unless they are raked and weeded regularly and given a top-dressing of fresh gravel every few years (gravel has a way of mysteriously disappearing) they tend to look very shabby. Gardening is not the same as housekeeping and tidiness is not the whole point of the exercise – but an ordered, weed-free look is very good for morale if other things aren't going as well as they should.

All paths can be kept clear of weeds with a flamegun but it must be used with discretion near the edges of paths, otherwise the foliage of nearby plants will suffer. Traffic – your feet or barrow wheels – keeps down weeds pretty well. A path that is persistently more weedy than others may not be used enough to justify its existence.

Don't hoe gravel paths. It breaks up the mixture of hard core and gravel underneath. The desired state is a very hard base, inhospitable to plants, with a loose, well-stirred cover that is equally inhospitable. This means use a rake and use it a lot.

The other way to keep paths clean (apart from Kipling's 'broken dinner knives') is to use a weedkiller. The least dangerous is sodium chlorate. It has been used a long time, seems to do little harm to the environment, apart from killing plants you don't want, and has no long-term side-effects that I know of. However, it is a poison and as such should be treated with great respect. Handle it with rubber gloves and use a watering can that you will never use for anything else. Sodium chlorate is a total weedkiller, it makes no exceptions. Nothing will grow in soil that has been treated with it for six months or more. Once in the soil, it can move sideways and be taken up by plants which then die. So don't use too near plants that you value. Don't splash it about on impervious surfaces. It will simply flow off and kill whatever is growing at the edge. Dead plants killed by sodium chlorate are highly inflammable. When buying it read carefully what it says on the tin. It may say that the mixture also contains atrazine or 2,4-D. These are poisons on a wholly different plane of nastiness and you should have nothing to do with them.

A second weedkiller, which can be cautiously recommended, is ammonium sulphamate, which is sold as *Amcide*. This is another total weedkiller which can kill trees. However, after a certain period in the soil it changes its chemical nature and becomes sulphate of ammonia, a common nitrogenous fertilizer. Land treated with *Amcide* is unsafe for planting for twelve weeks.

Bearing all this in mind, do think carefully if you are considering making a path. If you want to avoid years of irritating work, make it out of concrete, as solidly as you can. Concrete isn't pretty but you can vary the look of it by exposing the aggregate at the surface with a stiff brush when it's half-way dry. It weathers eventually. Don't have a gravel path in the vegetable garden. Nothing is more damaging to them than the lumps of soil and manure deposited on them by boots and wheels.

TAKE A PICTURE FOR POSTERITY

I have stressed elsewhere the value of a well-filled notebook. A few photographs can add greatly to its worth. They will remind you, when you are halfway through the job of construction and you think the place looks worse than ever, of what it looked like before you started.

5
THE FIRST YEAR

This chapter does not set out to tell you all that is to be known about growing vegetables, fruit and flowers; but it will, I hope, tell you how to get the best out of your new or rescued garden in its first year of cultivation. You must not expect everything to happen at once. Creating a garden takes time as well as hard work and new things always look raw. But you can be quite sure that at the end of this first year, if you have cultivated conscientiously and allowed no weed to raise its head, the real hard work will be over.

What to Grow?
There is an easy answer to this question, which is, nothing permanent. You may think you have dug out all the weeds but you can be perfectly certain that there are enough lurking underground to make life unpleasant later on. There is absolutely no point in paying, say, three or four pounds for an apple tree and then have it choked by couch grass before it has been in the ground six months. The same applies equally to shrubs and herbaceous plants. I think this cautious attitude will be of particular value to new gardeners. In the first year of gardening many mistakes are made and many misconceptions destroyed. It is less painful if this process occurs as cheaply as possible, and there is hardly anything cheaper than a packet of annual flower seeds.

Vegetables
Some vegetables, notably potatoes, are sometimes described as 'cleaning crops'. This needs some explanation. Quite simply, it isn't the potatoes that do the cleaning (although their dense canopy of leaves does help to blot small annual weeds late in the season) all by

themselves. You do it, because the cultivation they require demands so much sweat and hard work. In this sense, all crops are cleaning crops if you hoe them as they ought to be hoed.

At the risk of being boring, I would like to repeat that the greatest problem in a new or rescued garden is weeds. You may be very lucky and have clean ground, but the chances are that in the first spring your newly-cultivated ground will sprout weeds incessantly. These fearsome growths will very quickly choke any seedling vegetables among them. This often happens to root vegetables sown early in the year, in February or March.

For instance, the advice generally given is to sow parsnips in February. Perhaps you can get away with this if you live on the south coast and want roots as long and as thick as your arm; but elsewhere, the seedlings will take an age to appear and forests of weed seedlings will be ahead of them in the race for light, moisture and nutrients. So, wait until a flush of weeds indicates that the ground is warming up, destroy the weeds with a hoe and then sow your seed. If you want to be extra thorough, wait until you have destroyed a second flush. April-sown parsnips are quite big enough for the average sized family.

Another advantage of sowing later is that the seed germinates and grows swiftly without the checks imposed by late frosts and even snow showers. You can apply this technique to all root vegetables and to anything else that can be sown where it is to grow. Of course, you will miss early vegetables this way, but it's better than having no vegetables at all.

Another valuable technique, but an expensive one, is to make the drills for root crops much deeper and wider than the usual half inch (15mm) groove. Make them two inches (5cm) deep and fill them with a sterile medium, like granulated peat or seed sowing compost and sow your seed in a little drill drawn in the top of it. This ensures that the seedlings will grow up in a weed-free strip two inches wide, where they can easily be spotted and thinned as necessary.

Some vegetables usually sown where they are to grow can be transplanted. These include all beans, peas if you have the patience to produce so many little plants in pots, sweet corn and onions. These, and even the vegetables sown to be transplanted (the vast cabbage tribe, leeks, tomatoes, cucumbers and marrows), are best sown in trays and boxes, in sterilized potting compost. The usual advice is to

THE FIRST YEAR

sow cabbages and the like in a seed bed out of doors, but if you have dirty ground and no way of sterilizing it the seedlings are likely to be choked, especially if they are sown as early in the year as some of them, for instance Brussels sprouts, need to be.

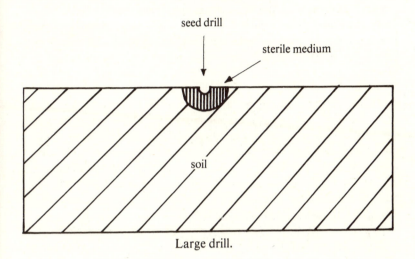

Large drill.

Sowing in Pots and Seed Trays

As you have gone to the trouble of buying expensive sterilized compost, make sure that the pots are absolutely clean. Scrub them and wash them as carefully as you would a dinner-plate. A fish-tailed washing-up brush is the ideal instrument. Next, cover the drainage hole with a few washed crocks (pieces of broken clay pot) or a layer of clean flat stones. Cover the crocks with a layer of fibrous material, like coarse peat, or torn up pieces of clean turf. Finally, put in your seed compost, leaving a good inch (2.5cm) clear for watering. Peat-based composts are best firmed lightly with the fingers. John Innes composts, which are loam-based, can be firmed and made even with a smooth flat piece of wood. Next, place the tray in a bowl of clean, tepid water, just up to the lip of the tray, but not beyond. Wait until the surface of the compost darkens with moisture and set the tray aside to drain for several hours. This is a more thorough method of watering than using a can (you can use just as well when the seedlings are growing) and is kinder to the structure of the compost.

Now sow the seeds, generally about half an inch (1.5cm) apart. Make sure your hands are dry when doing this job and place each seed individually. Using tweezers might make this easier for you. Cover the seeds by sifting compost over them. You need the same depth of compost as the largest dimension of the seed, no more. Cover with a piece of clean glass or place in a clear polythene bag and put the pots or trays on a well-lighted window sill or in a cold frame. Remove the glass or bag as soon as the seedlings show.

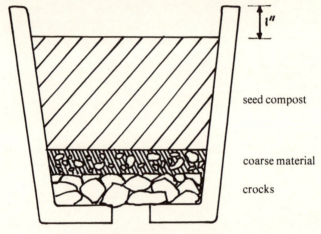

Pot filled for sowing.

When the seedlings have well-developed seed-leaves, prick them out (that is, transplant them) into larger trays or into small individual pots. Take care over this job. Never handle a seedling by the stem, unless you want to kill it. Always take them by the very tip of the leaf. At this stage you can decide how many plants you want. For instance, twenty-four of a good variety of Brussels sprouts should be enough for a family of four with hearty appetites. Of course, if you are sowing any of the cabbage family in March or after you won't have to put the tray in a cold frame. Any sheltered place outside will do.

If all this strikes you as too much trouble just for cabbages, then sow them outside on a seedbed, but don't do this casually. Start the job of preparation a month before you intend to sow. Fork the ground thoroughly and leave it rough for the wind and sun to dry it out. Then break it down with a cultivator and rake. Use the rake intelligently, rake back and forth, pushing and pulling. You will remove stones, of course, but the clods should be broken down, not just raked off. If they don't break down, wait a few more drying days until they do. The next thing to do is to wait. You have, we hope, created a perfect seed bed in which weed seeds will germinate with enthusiasm. Kill them when they do.

Next, firm the ground by trampling up and down, flat-footed. If the soil sticks to your boots, stop: the ground is still too damp. Having firmed the bed, rake it once more and make your drills, six inches (15cm) apart for the cabbage tribe, onions and leeks. You can do this with a pointed stick or by laying the handle of your rake across the bed and treading it into the surface to a depth of half an inch (1.5cm). This last method is the best as it ensures a perfectly even depth of sowing.

Alternatively, you can (as I suggested above) make extra-large drills filled with sterile compost.

Try to sow thinly. If you cannot manage this make sure that you thin the seedlings as soon as they appear, no later. With onions and leeks half an inch on either side is enough, with the cabbage tribe, one and a half inches (4cm) on either side is better. Crowded seedlings don't develop well and suffer much more from root damage when they are moved.

Transplanting

Transplant carefully. Give the plants a good drink twenty-four hours before, so they can withstand the shock better. With pot-grown plants, make your hole with a trowel slightly deeper than the pot is high, so that there is a slight depression that will retain the post-planting water. Take the pot in your left hand by the rim, with the stem of the plant between, but definitely not gripped by, the index and middle fingers. There is no need to touch either stem or leaf. Now, hold the base of the pot with your right hand and invert it, giving the rim a sharp knock against something firm, like the toe of your boot. The plant with its ball of roots will come cleanly out of the pot and sit, roots up, in the palm of your left hand. Taking care not to damage the root ball, put it in the hole and fill in the sides with fine soil. Make it firm with your fingers or the butt of your trowel. Water it well.

Plants grown in a seed-bed need even more care. Dig them up with a fork put in wide of the row. You want as much root as possible. Dig up only as many as you can plant in thirty minutes. Use a trowel to make the holes. A dibber should be used only for leeks and onion sets. Choose a cool day for transplanting, if possible, when rain is on the way. If the weather turns dry and windy, you must shade the plants and give them plenty of water. Shade with anything – inverted plant pots and boxes are handy. A flagging plant needs help and should be shaded and watered until its leaves can stand up on the brightest day.

Planting Distances
In dirty ground the safest thing to do is to give plants plenty of space. This means that you can always get between them with a hoe. Never broadcast seeds, sow them in the straightest lines you can, so you know where they should come up. Unfortunately, this means that you cannot, at least for a few years, use the modern bed system of cultivation, which is by far the more productive. Until you are sure your ground is clean, you'll have to use the more old-fashioned system of widely-spaced drills.

Crop rotations
You should never grow one sort of vegetable for more than one year on the same piece of ground. There are good reasons for this. Firstly, different plants take different nutrients from the soil – if you grow the same plant on the same soil for too long, the nutrients become exhausted and the plants suffer. Secondly, this practice allows the pests and diseases peculiar to a particular crop to build up to epidemic levels. Hence insecticides, fungicides and all the other horrors of modern arable farming. If you rotate the crops, pests and diseases starve for want of a host. Cabbage root flies do not eat potatoes, potato blight does not affect cabbages.

The rotation most commonly used these days is a simple three-course one which ensures that there is always a two year gap before a crop returns to a particular piece of ground. It is given in detail in the table below.

Note that in the table, the brassicas (cabbages, etc.) always follow the peas and their relations. This is because peas add nitrogen to the soil by means of little nodules (easily visible) on their roots. Brassicas have a particular need for nitrogen, which promotes vigorous leaf growth. You will also note that the roots are not mucked. This is usual because muck tends to make roots fork, making them rather difficult to prepare for the kitchen. However, if it is weight of crop that you want muck them as heavily as possible. Some roots certainly will be forked but the rest will resemble artillery shells.

THREE-COURSE CROP ROTATION

First year	must muck	muck if you can	no muck
	brassicas (lime), potatoes, onions, leeks, celery.	all peas and beans, spinach, lettuce and salads.	roots.
Second year	no muck	must muck	muck if you can
	roots.	brassicas (lime), potatoes, onions, leeks, celery.	all peas and beans, spinach, lettuce and salads.
Third year	muck if you can	no muck	must muck
	all peas and beans spinach, lettuce and salads.	roots.	brassicas (lime), potatoes, onions, leeks, celery.

Although brassicas and potatoes are grouped together as needing muck, they have differing needs for lime. Lime the ground intended for brassicas, but definitely not that set aside for potatoes.

CULTURAL NOTES FOR VEGETABLES

As I said before, this chapter does not pretend to be all-knowing about vegetables, so the following notes are intended only as a brief guide.

Potatoes
This is the crop most often grown in new gardens but it seems to be treated with something like contempt — it's only the humble spud after all. The truth is, it needs just as much attention as any other vegetable, in fact, rather more than most. Order and obtain seed as early as possible after the New Year. Set the tubers on their ends in boxes, and leave them in a cool, light, frost proof place. This is to induce

sprouting. Sprouted seed always produces a much larger crop. Don't force growth by giving them heat. Shoots longer than three-quarters of an inch (2cm) are vulnerable when planted out. Plant out in the spring (I'm afraid I can't be more definite than that: watch your neighbours and follow their example). Set the tubers, sprouts uppermost, in drills 6 inches (15cm) deep. Early sorts should be set 12 inches (30cm) apart in drills, 24 inches (60cm) apart. These distances are greater than those usually given so that you can use your hoe more effectively. When the foliage is perhaps 6 to 9 inches high (16-25cm) you can start to earth up. Loosen the soil in between the rows with a cultivator or fork then draw the soil up the potato stems with a draw hoe or a rake. Do this several times during the season. The potatoes develop in the loose soil of the ridges. Lift the crop as soon as the foliage dies and store in loosely closed sacks in a frost-proof shed.

Root Vegetables (Carrots, parsnips, beetroot, swedes and turnips)
Sow these where they are to grow in shallow drills 15 inches apart (40cm) from March to June. Late May is quite early enough to sow main crop carrots and swedes. Lift and store roots in the autumn. Store as potatoes. Parsnips may be left in the ground. Frost improves their flavour.

Onions
Beginners or anyone living north of the Wash, should plant onion sets in rows 15 inches (40cm) apart with 6 inches (15cm) between each of the little bulbs. Don't bury the bulbs; the tip should just show. Sow onion seed as for root crops no more than $\frac{1}{4}$ inch (1cm) deep. Harvest in September when the tops turn yellow and fall over. Hang them up in bunches in an airy shed. The smallest keep longest.

Leeks
Sow on a seedbed out of doors or in pots in March. Transplant in early June 9 inches (25cm) apart in rows 15 inches (40cm) apart. Make a hole with a dibber, put the leek in and water it heavily. The water will wash fine soil about its roots. Earth them up if you want long white stems.

Celery

Only to be grown if you are prepared to treat it well. It likes muck and endless water. The seed should be sown in heat in March, pricked out into boxes and transplanted 12 inches (30cm) apart into prepared trenches in June. Previously, the trenches have been dug out two spades wide and a spit deep. Dig muck into the bottom. Start earthing up the celery in August and September. Wrap up the stems in corrugated paper. Slugs are the desperate enemy of celery. Make traps for them up and down the trench. Use a board or a tile propped up slightly with a stone and bait it with something irresistible, like a fresh lettuce leaf. You will find slugs under the plank early in the morning. Or set saucers filled with sweetened beer. The slugs will plunge to an alcoholic death.

Peas

As I have explained, peas can be transplanted, but usually they are sown from February to June in 9 inch (25cm) wide drills. The drills should be 2 inches (5cm) deep. Place the seed carefully, about 2 inches (5cm) apart across the full width of the drill. If you are growing several rows together, the intervals between should be equal to the final height of the peas. Support all peas, even the smallest. Use brushwood, netting or canes and twine. Plastic netting is a good investment.

Runner Beans

Sow in pots or at the foot of 6 foot (2m) poles set 1 foot (30cm) apart at the end of May. Not a crop for cold districts. Make sure your framework of poles is sound. Once well-covered with foliage it will be vulnerable to high winds.

French Beans

Sow in the same way as runners but don't provide support. A good gap filler.

Broad Beans

One of the hardiest vegetables. The earliest crops are sown in October or November of one year, left to stand for the winter and harvested in June or July of the following year. Later crops are sown in March.

Sow in a double row, each seed 9 inches (25cm) from its fellow. Two inches (5cm) is deep enough. Support with canes and twine.

Summer and Autumn Cabbage
Sow in pots or boxes or on a seedbed from February onwards. Different varieties mature at different times but they are all grown the same way. Transplant when the plants have made six leaves. Early varieties need no more than 15 inches (40cm) all round. Later varieties like a little more room. Watch out for cabbage white butterflies and their caterpillars. Derris will kill them safely, but so will your finger and thumb.

Cauliflowers
These are more demanding than cabbages. They need a rich soil and careful treatment. Sow and transplant as for cabbages and give them 2 feet (60cm) all round in their final position. Most varieties need to be sown at the right time if they are to mature at the right time. Consult a seed catalogue.

Sprouting Broccoli
Late April is early enough to sow this crop, either in a seedbed or in pots. Transplant to 2 feet (60cm) all round. In the autumn, earth up the stems to prevent the wind rocking them out.

Kale
The hardiest greens. Sow and plant as for broccoli.

Brussels Sprouts
Sow in the same way as the other brassicas but as early as you can, in late February or early March. Transplant to 2 feet (60cm) all round. Late, tall varieties need more room. Earth up and stake the plants for the winter.

Spring Cabbage
Sow in July or August and transplant in September, at about 15 inches (40cm) all round. Don't feed them before the winter. You want hardly little plants that will survive frost. Harvest in June.

Marrows
Sow in small pots in late May, two seeds in a pot, and discard the latecomer when it appears. Plant out in rich soil when all danger of frost is past. Trailing marrows need much more room than the bush types. I don't mention courgettes under a separate heading. The small fruit of any marrow plant can quite rightly be called a courgette.

Spinach
So far I have refrained from stating my own preferences but in the case of spinach I strongly suggest you sow only one kind – spinach beet. Unlike ordinary spinach, one sowing will last the summer and autumn. Sow in the same way as roots.

Lettuce
Until May, lettuce can be transplanted, after that, sow them where they are to grow or they will bolt. The crisphead and cos varieties are best for summer weather, the butterheads for the rest of the year. Sow them a little and often and give them 12 inches (30cm) all round.

Radish
The easiest vegetable to grow. Don't set aside space for it. A few inches here and there will provide all you need. Use radish seeds as markers in rows of slower germinating seeds. They will show where the rows are and will be eaten before they can compete with their host.

Flowers
This means annuals. Keep the perennials for later years when you have got things in order. The number of annuals you could grow is enormous, so the following list is confined to the easy and the absolutely hardy. You can sow them in pots, on seedbeds or where they are to grow. As with vegetables, don't be in too much of a hurry if you are sowing *in situ*. Wait for a few weeds to appear and kill them before you sow.

Calendula	Cornflower	Sunflowers
Candytuft	Godetia	Phacelia
Chrysanthemum	Larkspur	Shirley poppies
Clarkia	Nasturtium	Opium poppies

Fighting the Weeds

Throughout the growing season, keep your hoe in constant motion. You should try to move every inch of the surface of your plot once every week or ten days. Hoe even where there seems to be no new growth — you can be sure that weed seeds are germinating every day and that each time you disturb the soil you kill some and induce still more to germinate. Each time you chop the top of some couch grass or ground elder you weaken it. Plants must have light for photosynthesis. If you chop off the leaves, the process cannot take place and in the end, the plant must starve and die. I cannot pretend that this is anything other than a slow process, but if you keep your hoe moving you will win.

Hoeing

Keep your hoe sharp enough to cut your finger. A quick rub with a file before you start work makes all the difference.

Everyone works in the way that suits them best, so I cannot lay down firm rules about how to hoe. However, as a rough guide, this is how I would hoe a bed of onions. Assume the onions are planted out in rows 15 inches (40cm) apart. As the bed is on a slope and I am right-handed, I start at the bottom left-hand corner. Straddling the first row (I tread on few leaves this way) I work my way up the row hoeing the area between the plants, but ignoring the area between the rows. I use a short-handled onion hoe. At the top of the row, I walk down to the bottom of the hill and start again. This is because I don't like bending too much and it's much harder work downhill. Of course, if the bed were level, I wouldn't bother. When I am finished, at the top right hand corner, I take my Dutch hoe and work my way backwards down the row, straddling it, as usual. And so on, back to the bottom left hand corner. This method takes time but it leaves no soil, or weed, undisturbed. No cut weeds are trodden in by my boots to root and grow again.

For heavier work, such as tackling well-established weeds, a draw hoe is more suitable. It copes better with heavier soils as well. Unfortunately, it is best used walking forwards, so that the ground is left trodden.

Heavy Mulches

In the long term, and especially under soft fruit and shrubs, weeds are best controlled with heavy mulches. A mulch is a thick layer of loose organic matter laid round plants. Not only does it suppress weeds, it also feeds the plant and conserves moisture over its roots. Before you apply a mulch, make sure the ground is free of perennial weeds. These materials are the perfect medium – moist and open-textured – through which ground elder and couch grass can make lightning progress. Once weeds have a hold in a mulch, you have a problem, because the mulch impedes the hoe.

Usual materials include compost, manure, straw, sawdust and bark. The first two can be used as they come but the last three must be supplemented with a good top-dressing of dried blood or hoof and horn meal. This is because they are unrotted and the bacteria whose task it is to rot them down will draw much nitrogen from the soil – to the disservice of the plants. Straw comes in bales which break down into wads about 6 inches (15cm) thick. Don't break them but spread them as they are. Bark can be had for the asking at country saw mills. It's a very long lasting material. Sawdust can be had for nothing from joiner's workshops and sawmills.

All mulches should be laid thickly. Think of 6 inches (15cm) as a minimum.

You may have noticed that I have not mentioned one common material – peat. It is not that peat isn't excellent stuff, far from it. It is free of weed seeds, gives a good texture to the soil and looks beautiful when laid down. However, it is expensive if you are thinking of mulching a large area. Reserve it for use in potting composts and mulching precious ericaceous plants like rhododendrons and heaths.

6
FUTURE YEARS

After the first year of cultivation, there is no doubt that your ideas about the eventual shape and function of your garden will have changed. You will have found out about your physical capabilities and aptitudes and about how much time you really can afford to give to the garden. You will have started to develop a particular taste in flowers and will have found out that you like some vegetables much more than others; that you have grown far too much spinach and far too few peas; that some vegetables aren't worth the trouble of sowing them and that others repay almost any effort.

It's time to take stock again, refer to your notebooks and scribble out plans. Now is the time to do as much serious garden visiting as you can, so that you can see how the experts do it. Look in your local paper each weekend and look for a little paragraph giving details of gardens open to the public. Some of them will be very grand indeed but most will be quite small and more human in scale. Take a notebook and a pencil and write it all down. Take a camera as well, preferably loaded with colour film. Many plants will be labelled but if they are not, don't be afraid to get hold of the owner and ask. You may feel that you are showing appalling ignorance by doing so, but they don't care. Good gardeners never have secrets. They are willing to give a name to any plant, however common, or explain any technique, however obvious it may seem.

During your visits don't be tempted to steal cuttings. If you are really bold you can ask for a piece of the plant you covet. If the plant is rare and precious and throws very little cutting material, you will be refused. But you may be in luck and go home loaded with treasures.

Other sources of inspiration are catalogues. You will see them advertised at all seasons of the year. Get as many as you can.

Read books. You don't *have* to buy them; your public library is full of them. A surprising number of gardeners never read a book about their hobby. Don't be like them or you will miss a great deal of information and entertainment.

Shelter and Hedges
After the first year, experience will have shown you where the most damaging winds blow from. Now, with clean ground, you can think about creating permanent windbreaks. You can build a wall but it is not the best kind of shelter. When wind strikes a wall, an eddy is created which rises over the top and strikes the plants on the other side with scarcely diminished force. A hedge is best because it absorbs the energy of the wind and allows it to filter gently through.

A hedge should last a lifetime, so take care over planting it. Dig the ground well, remove the roots of perennial weeds and muck it if you can. When ordering plants, avoid the larger sizes, especially with conifers. A two year old plant is quite big enough. Older plants sometimes never recover from the shock of transplanting.

COMMON HEDGING PLANTS

Quickthorn
Not the best hedge for a suburban setting but quite definitely the best for the country. It is stock-proof, dense and only needs clipping once a year. Plant out in a staggered double row 18 inches (45cm) apart in the autumn and winter.

Beech
A handsome hedge. Plant in winter in a staggered double row, 2 to 3 feet (60-90cm) apart. Clip in June.

Yew
By far the best-looking hedge. The perfect background for plants. Manure it well and it will grow quicker than you expect. Plant in winter, in a single row, 3 feet (90cm) apart. Clip in July.

Lawson's Cypress
Evergreen. Plant either in September or April 2 to 3 feet apart (60-90cm). Trim in June with pruners rather than clippers.

Leyland Cypress
Evergreen and very fast growing. Plant 4 feet (120cm) apart in a single row in September or April. Clip in June.

Privet
This makes a dense, easily controlled hedge but it has the great drawback of being a gross feeder. Not much grows well, within three feet (90cm) of it. Plant in winter 2 feet (60cm) apart in a single row. Trim in May and July.

Having planted a hedge, take great care of it. Water it and weed it. Cut strong growing shoots back hard. This will promote the dense growth you want. When clipping the hedge, don't make the very common mistake of undercutting it, so that the top is wider than the bottom. This deprives the lower leaves of light and eventually the bottom of the hedge dies right back.

Fences
A fence isn't much of a windbreak unless it's clothed in expensive wind-cheating plastic net and then it looks grey and drab. However, clothed with the right kind of climbing plant, a fence can be a windbreak and productive too. Good fruit to grow on a fence include the cultivated brambles and the hybrid berries, like loganberries. A grapevine can cover a lot of space. In more favourable districts, plant the variety 'Brandt' which has handsome leaves in the autumn as well as small grapes.

For a purely ornamental hedge, plant clematis. *Clematis tangutica* with tiny lemon flowers or *Clematis montana*, with white or pink flowers are two good ones easily obtainable. The more vigorous climbing roses such as 'Mermaid' make a good screen but like the cultivated brambles they need training and tying in. For the ultimate in vigour and covering power, plant the impossibly named *Polygonum baldschuanicum* – the Russian vine. This will quite easily cover 50 or 60 feet (18m) of fence in a very few years. It produces lots of tiny cream white flowers in late summer. Watch out that it doesn't take over the entire garden.

Trees and Shrubs for the Future
When buying shrubs, do read the catalogue carefully. The best

catalogues will tell you what conditions suit a particular kind of shrub. Take this advice – a good nurseryman wants satisfied customers who will come back for more. Take note of the eventual size of the plant. A new shrub border can look a bare and desolate place because the new plants are relatively tiny. Don't be tempted, on this account, to plant them any closer together. You can fill the spaces with annuals and short-lived perennials grown from seed. There are so many different kinds of shrubs, that it is impossible in a book of this sort to make any kind of recommendation. But when it comes to planting trees I am prepared to push my personal view which is not to plant purely ornamental trees but to plant fruit. If there is room for only two or three trees in your garden (and this must be true of most gardens these days) let them be fruit trees. Fruit trees are no duller than the other trees simply because they have a use. An apple tree in blossom is a fine sight. And it's even finer in the autumn when loaded down with handsome fruit.

Planting Trees and Shrubs

I don't think there are any cheap trees and shrubs these days, so obviously you will regard them as an investment to be treated with especial care.

First of all, dig over the planting site and remove the weeds. Then do it again, removing all those weeds you missed the first time and digging in manure or compost, as you go. Dig your hole as wide and as deep as the roots of the plant extend. Don't dig a smaller hole and then force the roots to conform to it. Well-spread roots provide a firm anchorage and are not obliged to compete with their fellows.

If you are planting a tree that will need a stake, this is the time to put it in. Be sure it's at least 2 inches (5cm) square and that the bottom end has been treated with horticultural wood preservative – not creosote, which would probably kill the tree. Next, try the tree for fit. If it's right, hold it in one hand at the correct level in the hole. You can easily determine this by laying a stick from side to side across the hole. You will see a darkening – the soil-mark – on the stem of the tree. Plant the tree at this level, sifting the soil with your hand carefully about the roots. Give the stem an occasional shake to settle the soil. When all the roots are well covered, firm the soil. Don't just stamp on the soil in the hole. Straighten your leg, make it stiff as a post and lean on it, applying pressure through the heel. This is a far more effective method.

Fill the depression with water. When it has drained away replace the last of the soil and apply a mulch of compost or manure. Tie the stem to its stake with a patent expanding tie or, much cheaper, an old pair of tights. Make sure that the stake and the stem aren't touching. Damage to the bark at this stage could be fatal. In future years, look at the tie to see if it needs adjusting. Most trees will soon grow beyond needing a stake but others, notably apples grown on dwarfing stocks, will need a stake all their lives.

SOME USEFUL ADDRESSES

Seedsmen

Samuel Dobie and Son Ltd.
Upper Dee Mills
Clwyd LL20 8SD

Thompson and Morgan (Ipswich) Ltd.
London Road
Ipswich
Suffolk IP2 OBA

Chase Compost Seeds Ltd.
Benhall
Saxmundham
Suffolk

Nurserymen

For shrubs and herbaceous plants:
Bressingham Gardens
Bressingham Hall
Diss
Norfolk

For fruit:
W. Seabrook and Sons Ltd.
Boreham
Chelmsford
Essex CM3 3AE

Organizations Promoting Organic Farming and Gardening
The Soil Association
Walnut Tree Manor
Haughley
Stowmarket
Suffolk

The Henry Doubleday Research Association
Convent Lane
Bocking
Braintree
Essex

FURTHER READING

The Vegetable Garden Displayed
The Fruit Garden Displayed
Both published by the Royal Horticultural Society.
Grow Your Own Fruit and Vegetables by L.D. Hills (Faber and Faber).
Fruit Growing by H.G. Witham Fogg (John Gifford Ltd.).
Basic Gardening by Stanley B. Whitehead (J.M. Dent).
Hardy Herbaceous Plants by L. Roper (Penguin).
The Well-Tempered Garden by Christopher Lloyd (Collins).

INDEX

Agricultural Development and Advisory Service, 18, 66
Amcide, 72
Ammonium sulphamate, 72
Apples, 70, 73
   see also Fruit
Ash trees, 24
Aspect of plots, 12

Bark, use of in mulching, 85
Barrows, *see* Tools
Beans
   broad, 11, 81
   french, 81
   runner, 81
Beech, 24, 87
Beetroot, 80
'Big bud', 17
Billhooks, *see* Tools
Birch trees, 24
Blackcurrants, 9, 17
Blood, dried, 85
Bracken, 9-10
Brambles, 17, 67
   Himalaya Giant, 17
   cultivated, 88
Brassicas, 74, 76, 77, 78-9
Broccoli, 82
Brussels sprouts, 36, 75, 76, 82
Buckets, *see* Tools
Buttercups, 16

Cabbages, 15, 23, 25-6, 75, 82
Cabbage family, *see* Brassicas
Cabbage root flies, 78
Calendula, 83
Candytuft, 83
Carnations
   Crimson Clove, 17
   Nutmeg Clove, 17
Cauliflowers, 82
Chrysanthemums, 59, 83
Clarkia, 83
Clays, 18, 20, 23, 26
Clematis
   wild, *see* Old man's beard
   clematis tangutica, 86
   clematis montana, 88
Clippers, 11
Clover, 24
Compost, 8, 9, 10, 19, 52, 53-5, 85, 89
   activators, 54
   building of heap, 55
   John Innes, 75
   materials for, 54
   potting, 59, 74, 77
   siting of heap, 54-5
Conifers, 24, 69
Cornflower, 83
Cottage gardens, 16
Couch grass, 11, 68, 73, 85
Crop rotation, 78-9
Cucumbers, 74
Cultivators, *see* Tools
Cypress
   Lawson's, 87
   Leyland, 88

Dandelions, 8, 52
Dibbers, 78
Digging, 33, 57-60
 double digging, 59-60, 65
 single digging, 57-8
Docks, 11
Dogwood, 24
Drainage, 9, 16, 64-7
Drives, care of, 71-2

Edging irons, 11
Elderberry, 18
Engines
 diesel, 46
 four-strokes, 44-5
 petrol, 44
 starting techniques, 45-6
 two-strokes, 44

Fences, 88
Fens, 19
Fertility, 19
Fertilizers
 artificial, 8
 organic, 8
Flameguns, see Tools
Flocculation, 23
Forks, see Tools
Foxgloves, 24
Fruit, 13, 17, 70, 85, 89
Fungicides, 78
Furzes, 24

Gall mites, 17
Geraniums, hardy, 69
Goats, 52
Godetia, 83
Grapevine, 88
Grass-hooks, see Tools
Gravels, 22
Ground elder, 68, 85
Groundsel, 52
Gypsum, 26

Heathers, 24
Heaths, 85

Hedge clippers, see Tools
Hedges, 9, 15, 41, 70, 87-8
Hens, 64
Herbaceous borders, 68-9
Herbicides, see Weed killers
Herbs, 17
Hoes, see Tools
Hoof and horn, 85
Humus, 19, 22, 52, 58
Hydrated lime, 26

Insecticides, 78
Interception ditch, 66-7
Irrigation, 15

Kale, 82

Lake District, 9
Land tiles, 16, 66
Larkspur, 83
Lavender, 17, 70
Lawns, 67
Leeks, 74, 77, 80
Lettuce, 87
Lifting, techniques of, 31-2
Lime, 10, 23, 24, 26, 79
Loam, 18, 22, 23, 59
Loganberries, 88
Loppers, see Tools
Lupins, 69

Manure, 8, 19, 23, 30, 34, 89
Marjoram, 17
Marrows, 74
Mattocks, see Tools
Measuring
 equipment, 50
 methods of, 12, 55-6
Michaelmas daisies, 68, 69
Ministry of Agriculture, 70
Mints, 17
Mowing machines, see Tools
Mulching, 70, 85
Mushroom growing, 26

Nasturtiums, 83

INDEX

Nettles, 11
   remedy for stings of, 30

Old man's beard, 24
Onions, 74, 77, 80, 84
Organic gardening, 8
Outside water supply, 16

Parsnips, 74, 80
Paths, 9, 10, 71-2
Pears, 70
Peas, 36, 74, 81, 86
Peat, 70, 75, 85
   granulated, 74
Peat moors, 24
Peonies, 68
Pesticides, 8
pH, 24, 25
Phacelia, 83
Photosynthesis, 84
Pickaxes, *see* Tools
Pigs, 63-4
Planting distances, 78
Plough pan, 20
Polygonum baldschuanicum, 88
Poppies
   Shirley, 83
   opium, 83
Potatoes, 26, 34, 68, 69, 73, 78, 79
Potato blight, 78
Pots, 75-6
Power saws, *see* Tools
Primroses
   Quakeress, 17
   Mme de Pompadour, 17
Pruners, *see* Tools
Pruning, 69, 70
Pumpkins, 59

Quickthorn, 87

Radishes, 83
Rainfall, 9, 15
Rakes, *see* Tools
Raspberries, 17
Rhododendrons, 24, 69, 85

Roses, climbing, 88
Rotavation, 61-3
Rotavators, *see* Tools
Rubbish, making use of, 56
Rushes, 16
Russian vine, *see Polygonum baldschuanicum*

Sage, 17
Sands, 18, 22, 23
Sawdust, use of in mulching, 85
Saws, *see* Tools
Scab, 26
Scythes, *see* Tools
Sea-level, height above, 13
Seed trays, use of, 74, 75
Septic tanks, 11, 16
Shovels, *see* Tools
Shrubs, 69-70, 73, 85, 88-90
   pruning of, 69
Sickles, *see* Tools
Slope, advantages and disadvantages of, 13
Slugs, 81
Sodium chlorate, 71
Soil
   acidity of, 24
   alkalinity of, 24
   assessment of, 18, 21
   fertility of, 8
   profile, 19
   subsoil, 7, 10, 20, 59
   testing kits, 24
   top soil, 7, 10, 19, 20
   types, 22-3
Sowing, 75-6
Sow thistle, 51-2
Spades, *see* Tools
Spinach, 83, 86
Spring cabbages, 11
Standing water, 16
Straw, use of in mulching, 85
Strawberries, 17, 70
Sumps, 66
Sunflowers, 83
Swedes, 80

Sweet corn, 74

Thyme, 17
Tomatoes, 59, 74
Tools, 27-50
  barrows, 37
  billhooks, 41-2
  buckets, 38
  cultivators, 36, 77
  flameguns, 49-50, 52
  forks, 34, 67, 68, 69, 70, 76, 78
  grass-hooks, 40-41
  hedge clippers, 43
  hiring of, 27-8
  hoes, 36, 68, 71, 74, 84
    'Chillington', 37
  loppers, 42
  mattocks, 35
  mowing machines, 48
  pickaxes, 35
  power saws, 48
  pruners, 42
  rakes, 10, 36, 67, 71, 77
  rotavators, 10, 30, 47-8, 61
  saws, 43-4

scythes, 38-40, 52
shovels, 34-5
sickles, 10, 41
slashers, 41-2
spades, 32-3, 57
Tractors, 63
Transplanting, 76
Trenches, 16
Turf, 9, 10, 11, 59, 63, 66
Turnips, 80

Vegetables, 73-5

Water rights, 16
Weeds, 8, 10, 11, 16, 38, 50, 51, 52, 57, 58, 59, 68, 69, 70, 71, 73, 74, 77, 83, 84, 85, 89
Weedsheets, 38
Wet ground, 16
Wind
  prevailing, 13, 87
  problem of, 9, 15
Windscreens, 15, 88
Worms, 19
Yew, 87